RULES
for Revolutionaries

Also by Guy Kawasaki

Hindsights
Selling the Dream
The Macintosh Way
Database 101
The Computer Curmudgeon
How to Drive Your Competition Crazy

RULES
for Revolutionaries
The Capitalist Manifesto for Creating and Marketing New Products and Services

Guy Kawasaki

with Michele Moreno

HarperBusiness
An Imprint of HarperCollinsPublishers

A hardcover edition of this book was published in 1999 by HarperBusiness, an imprint of HarperCollins Publishers.

First paperback edition published 2000.

Designed by Nancy Singer Olaguera

The Library of Congress has catalogued the hardcover edition as follows:
Kawasaki, Guy, 1954–
    Rules for Revolutionaries : the capitalist manifesto for creating and marketing new products and services / Guy Kawasaki with Michele Moreno. — 1st ed.
    p. cm.
    Includes bibliographical references and index.
    ISBN 0-88730-996-8
    1. New products. 2. Product management. I. Moreno, Michele. II. Title.
HF5415.153.K384   1999
658.5'75—dc21   98-11636

ISBN 0-88730-995-X (pbk.)

00 01 02 03 04 ❖/RRD 10 9 8 7 6 5 4 3 2 1

To my mother and father,
Because they taught me how to think, act, and defy.

Create like a god.

Command like a king.

Work like a slave.

Brancusi

Contents

CONCLUSION

The *Rules for Revolutionaries* Internet mail list is an open forum to discuss the ideas presented in this book.

If you would like to join the mail list, please send an e-mail to: <rfr-on@lists.garage.com>.

Or, you can sign up manually at: <http://www.garage.com/mailingLists.shtml>.

Acknowledgments

Behind every successful author stands an amazed agent.

Guy Kawasaki

The concept of a solo author, writing passionately with the muse, may work for some people but not for me. I need a team to compensate for my weaknesses. This is the *Rules for Revolutionaries* team:

Visionaries. Bill Meade and John Michel. In the history of the printed word, no author has gotten better guidance than what I received from Bill and John. If you don't like something in this book, it's probably because I didn't listen to them.

Beta testers. Geoff Baum, Dave Brady, Julie Livingston, Steven Long, Russell Roberts, Charles Schrey, and Bobbi Silten. You should have seen the *drek* (AKA, drafts) that these folks had to read. You do see the quality of the changes they suggested.

Sources. Michele Moreno is the dream research assistant. She understands what I mean when I don't understand what I mean and can take the sketchiest of ideas and flesh them out. Suzanne C. Anthony, Nina Barclay, Holly Camerota, Steve Glasscock, Jodi Granston, Laurie Hill, Chris O'Leary (The Cyberdigm Group), Amy Stuhlberg, Carey Tews, Mark Thomashow, Stephanie Vardavas, Jon Winokur, and the 600 members of the Rules for Revolutionaries mailing list were fantastic assistance too. The breadth and depth of the examples in this book are attributable to the help of these lovely birds who pooped like elephants.

Evangelists. Jack Covert and Sebastian Ritscher. Jack, my main man in Milwaukee, paved the way for me at HarperCollins. Sebastian opened up Europe for me. *Domo arigato*, guys.

HarperCollins. Lisa Berkowitz, Adrian Zackheim, and Amy Lambo. My mother taught me to thank people who put their faith (and money) on the line for you. Lisa and Adrian, I thank you. Lisa, incidentally, is the only person who can call me "love" and get away with it. Also, thank you to John Day, Patricia Wolf, and the fine crew of production people who took my imperfections and turned them into a book.

Special. Brother Steve Corrick helped me name the book. Without him, I would have called it *How to Swim with the Bozos and Not Get Slimed* or *Only the Geeks Survive*. Finally there's Sloan Harris, my agent at International Creative Management. Truth be known, I was amazed that he (and ICM) would want a schlepper like me. Thank God he did, or I might be self-publishing. Keep bringing those editors to tears, Sloan baby, because when they're crying, we're getting rich.

Foreword

Here's to the crazy ones, the misfits, the rebels, the trou-
blemakers, the round pegs in a square hole, the ones
who see things differently. They're not fond of rules,
and they have no respect for the status quo. You can
quote them, disagree with them, glorify or vilify them.
About the only thing you can't do is ignore them,
because they change things. They push the human race
forward, and while some may see them as the crazy
ones, we see genius, because the people who are crazy
enough to think they can change the world, are the ones
who'll do it.

Apple Computer advertising, 9/27/97*

You may wonder—quite reasonably—how someone (me)
who has won his notoriety through fanatical devotion to a
troubled revolutionary company (Apple Computer) could write
a book about creating successful revolutions.

Short answer: Chutzpah.

Long answer: The best possible credential for the author of
this book is scar tissue from battling resistance to change.

I have plenty of scar tissue because I have been in the
trenches in two revolutionary wars: Macintosh and the
Internet. Now I wish to pass my knowledge and the mouse to

---

* <http://www.apple.com/>

the next generation of revolutionaries. This is the book that I wish I could have read at the beginning of my career.

Like Gaul*, *Rules for Revolutionaries* is divided into three sections.

Create like a god. This section explains how to create revolutionary products and services. Three chapters—each with a title that I stole—explain how to do this: Cogita Differenter ("Think different," Apple Computer's advertising theme); Don't Worry, Be Crappy (Bobby McFerrin's song, *Don't Worry, Be Happy*); and Churn, Baby, Churn ("Burn, baby, burn!" the slogan of the Black Panthers).

Command like a king. For a revolution to succeed, someone has to take charge and make the tough, insightful, and strategic decisions. Break Down the Barriers; Make Evangelists, Not Sales; and Avoid the Death Magnets (the stupid mistakes that just about everyone makes) explain what these decisions require.

Work like a slave. Successful revolutions require lots of hard work. In this section you'll learn the three most important components of that work: Eat Like a Bird, Poop Like an Elephant (trust me, this will make sense); Think Digital, Act Analog; and Don't Ask People to Do Something That You Wouldn't (this should already make sense).

There is no greater reward for an author than to see how people use his book to make the world a better place. May you have the creativity, courage, and conscientiousness to change the world for the better of all our children. And may you live in revolutionary, not merely interesting, times.

Guy Kawasaki
Kawasaki@garage.com

"Gallia est omnis divisa in partes tres." De Bello Gallico I, Julius Caesar.

PART 1

CREATE LIKE A GOD.

COMMAND LIKE A KING.

WORK LIKE A SLAVE.

1

Cogita Differenter (Think Different)[1]

I guess in all my years, what I heard more often than anything was: a town of less than 50,000 population cannot support a discount store for very long.

Sam Walton

The Shark Versus the Mouse

Since 1955 the Walt Disney Company* made the rules of the amusement park business. That's the year it opened Disneyland and set the standard for showmanship, efficiency, and profitability. Before Disneyland, the rule was that amusement parks needed big, scary roller-coasters to succeed. Disneyland changed all that by featuring *theme* rides instead of *thrill* rides.

For the next thirty years, amusement park companies played by Disney's rules, or they hardly mattered at all. And by playing by Disney's rules, they reinforced Disney's supremacy. Then along came Jay Stein. Jay Stein ran MCA Recreation,† the

---

*<http://www.disney.com/>

†<http://www.mca.com/>

company that owns Universal Studios—which includes the tourist activity Los Angelinos dread the most: the Universal Studios Tour. (Just how many times should a person have to endure the Parting of the Red Sea?)

Universal Studios was an also-ran in the amusement park business because it merely re-purposed content from the studio's main business of making movies. The rule it played by was simple and stupid: Stuff people on a tram, take them "behind the scenes" of a movie, drop them off, and hope they buy souvenirs.

But when MCA built Universal Studios Florida, Stein had a different idea of how to play the game. First, he threw out his own company's standard operating procedures. Instead of "See how we make the movies," his pitch became "Come ride the movies." *Back to the Future* (the movie), became *Back to the Future* (the ride). Where else can you ride in a time machine disguised as a DeLorean? Stein combined theme and thrill to rewrite Universal's rules.

But it gets better.

Next Stein went after the de facto rules established by Disney: Be nice, gentle, and politically correct. For example, the bleeding edge of Disneyland's rides is attractions like the Haunted Mansion and the Pirates of the Caribbean. They are works of art—far more "multimedia" than the vaunted multimedia efforts of the computer business—but not exactly risky.*

Stein decided that rides wouldn't be nice—instead, they would kick people's butts. So at Universal Studios Florida there are blood, guts, flames, and explosions. Every day there are customer complaints that the fireballs are too hot. The shark in the *Jaws* ride comes so close to the boat that it will break people's arms if they're dumb enough to put them in harm's way. And every day thousands of people come back for more.

There's not much that Disney can do about this full-frontal

---

*In 1996 Disneyland officials even decided that the pirates of Pirates of the Caribbean should chase the maidens for their baskets of food—not for sex. Being at sea for long periods of time can do that to you.

attack because it is a prisoner of its own G-rated, fun-but-safe standards and image. Stein used Aikido marketing:* turning the strengths of Disney into a constraining weakness. If Disney tried to liven up its rides, it would lose its core audience and blur its image.[2]

The Revolutionary Thought Process

Stein did what revolutionaries do: Think different in order to change the rules. By definition, if you don't change the rules, you aren't a revolutionary, and if you don't think different, you won't change the rules.

EXERCISE

Suppose you wanted to change the rules of the animated film business. How would you do it?

But how do revolutionaries come up with the insights that separate them from the crowd?

The conventional wisdom is that revolutionary ideas come to people after they contemplate a situation, condition, or problem for a long time. A more current and popular notion is that breakthrough insights and ideas appear when you're in the heightened, altered state of sitting in a beanbag chair squirting colleagues with water pistols.

But these observations are trite and not very helpful because coming up with a revolutionary idea is not simply a matter of thinking a long time (or shooting a water pistol). The key is *how* you are thinking about a problem for a long time. In fact, there are three key stages of the revolutionary thought process.

---

*Aikido marketing is using an opponent's strength against itself instead of meeting brute force with brute force. It gets its name from the Japanese martial art called Aikido that exploits an opponent's strength, weight, and motion.

Stage 1: Purge

The first step is purging—that is, disposing of old prejudices, procedures, and presuppositions that cloud and constrict your thinking. Perhaps evolution has programmed people to seek stability and safety, but revolution requires defiance of the status quo.

Dump your idols

Sir Francis Bacon was often aggravated because his contemporaries clung to existing ideas. He called these ideas "idols of the tribe, the den, the market, and the theater." They represent, respectively, the groupthink of a particular community, the qualities of a particular individual, the results of social interaction, and the drama of showing off one's intellectual prowess.[3]

Generally, idols spring up for good reason. Through experience we discover effective ways to avoid ghastly and stupid mistakes. However, success is habit-forming and creates rules, and fosters crowds that follow these rules. Over time the rules are not optimal or even applicable because the marketplace has changed. Or someone was just plain dumb lucky to begin with, so the rules should never have been established in the first place.

To make it easier to identify some of the idols that afflict you, your company, or your industry, here are some examples of foolish but generally accepted business practices:

- **Distribution idol:** "We sell through dealers. We don't sell to our customers directly."

- **Employee idol:** "Employees can't be trusted. We have to monitor their productivity and get after them when they're lax."

- **Market share idol:** "Market share causes profitability, so let's reduce prices to gain share."

- **Enemy idol:** "We can't cooperate with X Company because we compete with X Company."

Zero-based budgeting is the process in which every expense is questioned from the very first dollar—nothing is continued from previous budgets. "Zero-based idolizing," then, means questioning every business practice and trashing the ones that are no longer compelling. You cannot discard too many, so be ruthless!

EXERCISE

Create a list of the idols that your company worships. Then subject them to these questions:

- Why did this practice come to be?

- Is it still relevant?

- Most importantly, will it be relevant in the future?

The creation of Japan's bullet train illustrates how to analyze and discard idols. The challenge there was to create a transportation system that vastly reduced traveling time between cities. What idols might a train designer worship?

OLD IDOL	NEW THINKING
One car with an engine pulls the train	Put an engine in every car
The train needs a bigger engine to go faster	The sum total of the engines yields great power
The track should follow the topology of the terrain	Level the terrain to suit your purposes

The bullet train designers worshipped few idols. The concept of a train was radically changed: Every car had an electrically powered engine, and the tracks were laid in a straight line even if it involved plowing through mountains. In the end, the rules-busting bullet train cut the trip from Osaka to Tokyo from sixty-two hours down to three hours and ten minutes.[4]

Change the framing

> How do I love thee? Let me count the ways.
>
> *Elizabeth Barrett Browning*

Imagine the answer to the question above if it were posed this way: "What do you think of me?" How a question is posed limits the answers to that question. According to Massimo Piattelli-Palmarini, a researcher at MIT, "Hardly ever do we spontaneously alter the formulation of a problem that is presented to us in a reasonably clear and complete way."[5]

Piattelli-Palmarini calls this the "framing effect" because people try to solve a problem as it is presented. For example, consider the framing effect of the question, "How do we increase purchases by people shopping in our bookstore?" The unstated but crucial frame is that customers need to come to a physical bookstore.

A revolutionary refuses to solve problems as they are presented. Instead, a revolutionary uses thought processes like these:

- Consider the problem in the broadest context that's feasible.

- Start at the goal (more sales) and work backwards[6] (the next section contains more discussion of this technique).

- Do the opposite of the obvious answer.

Amazon.com* refused to be framed by the necessity of having a physical bookstore; instead it changed the rules of book selling. This company enables people to search through 2.5 million titles and then place their order electronically on its Web site. It has no physical storefront, and until 1998, it was

---

*<http://www.amazon.com/>

the only company that prevented "Internet commerce" from being an oxymoron.

FRAMED	UNFRAMED
Physical presence: bigger store, more books, more sales.	Cyber presence: no store, more books more sales.
Browse a book, read the jacket copy and blurbs, decide by yourself.	Read the reviews that have been posted by owners of the book or by the author.
Wait four to eight weeks for books not in stock.	Three- to five-day delivery for almost every order.
Make an impulse purchase because you picked up a book.	Make an impulse purchase because you read about it on a Web site.
Look on the shelf for a dozen or so books on related subjects.	Have a computer search through millions of books for related titles.

Interestingly, Amazon.com has allowed itself to be framed by the question, "How can we use price to compete?" and offers discounts that it doesn't have to. Oftentimes I feel so lucky to have found an old book from an obscure publisher that it's not necessary to also offer me a 10 percent discount. Instead of a reflexive dependency on price competition, Amazon.com should focus on ways to achieve sustainable differentiation from other booksellers.

Stage 2: Prod

Prodding is the second step of the revolutionary thought process. It means attacking challenges in ways that force you to consider new solutions and new courses of action.

Look for powerlessness

The Amazon.com example illustrates a powerful way to prod: Look for feelings like powerlessness, frustration, inconvenience, and pain—that is, what pisses people off? What pisses people off about traditional bookstores is that they are unlikely to have most books that aren't big sellers, and anything that isn't in stock takes four to eight weeks to order. This is the powerlessness, frustration, and pain (okay, maybe I'm exaggerating a little) that Amazon.com healed.

Separate form and function[7]

Sometime after the Gulf War, the Queen Mother of Oman fell ill and was treated at Walter Reed Army Medical Center. Because Oman was an ally, it was prudent for the United States to provide the best medical advice it could to this high-visibility patient.

Therefore, to provide continuity of care after her discharge, a telemedicine system was developed. This system linked the Royal Hospital in Muscat, Oman, to Walter Reed Army Medical Center* in Washington, D.C. It enabled the electronic transfer of medical information, including digitized medical images.

With computers and digital cameras on both ends, Army medical personnel at Walter Reed could "see" the patient in Oman as often as necessary. It was the first extended international telemedicine application, and from this initial experience, the concept was expanded for other military medical humanitarian missions.

The *form* of medical treatment is the face-to-face meeting of doctor and patient. The *function* of medical treatment is observation and diagnosis. Form and function are usually together at a medical facility where the doctor meets with a patient to perform the medical functions.

When you separate form from function, revolutionary pos-

---

*<http://www.hqda.army.mil/acsim/98direct/wramc.htm>

sibilities open up. In this case, the function remained the same: observation and diagnosis. The form, however, took on a new format: computers and high-speed networks between Oman and Walter Reed Army Medical Center.

Start at the goal and work backwards

One of the goals of a software company is fat, juicy margins. There are so many factors preventing this result that two-guys, two-gals, or a guy-and-a-gal in-a-garage (to cover every possible permutation) must change the rules of the game to survive.

One useful way is to start at the end result and work backwards. Working backwards from the customer, this is a list of the drains on profit margin of a software company. Is each one necessary?

- Discounts to stores or mail-order houses.

- Advertising co-op fees.

- Diskettes or CD-ROM duplication and media.

- Packaging and documentation.

- Shipping twice: first to a distributor who then ships it to a store.

- Office rent.

Star Games* is a "virtual" company on the Internet that is starting with the end result and working backwards. It is a game software company whose first product, Pacific Tide, is a simulation of the battles in the Pacific during World War II.

The game is for sale as a downloadable file on the Internet; thus, there are no discounts to stores or mail-order houses or advertising co-op fees. Copies of the game that are downloaded do not incur duplication or media costs. There is no packaging of these files, and documentation is a file that customers read

---

*<http://www.star-games.com/>

on their computer screens or print themselves.

Martin Favorite, the president, formed the company in 1995 by recruiting new employees on the Internet. As of 1997, there are fifteen employees, but Favorite has met only two of them face to face. Most of the employees work out of their homes. Translation: Less rent.

A simulation game of World War II requires extensive research. To do this research, Star Games was able either to enter the historical archives of several countries or to make friends with a local who did the research in exchange for a copy of the game—that is, a downloadable file!

Finally, Star Games can control marketing costs by using the resources of the Internet including links from Web sites dedicated to gaming, Internet mailing list servers and bulletin boards, and swapping advertising banner space with other Web sites.

Divide the problem into small parts[8]

Sometimes the size and complexity of a problem—particularly if you're trying to create a revolution—is so vast that you don't know where to start. The solution is to divide the problem into small parts and tackle the ones that are critical and haven't been solved.

For example, merely considering the totality of the challenge of flying probably condemned wannabe revolutionaries to failure. One of the shrewdest things Orville and Wilbur Wright did was to divide the problem into three pieces:

- Construction of wings.

- Generation and application of power.

- Balance and control once in flight.

By 1901 other inventors had solved the first two problems. People knew how to construct wings that could bear the weight of the plane, engine, and pilot, and engines had been designed that were powerful yet light enough for flight.

What distinguished the Wright brothers is that they focused on what it would take to *stay* aloft, not simply *get* aloft. Others continued to tinker with wings and engines, but the Wright brothers didn't waste time and money designing an airplane that was unstable after it took off. The critical issue was balance and control.

In theory, balance and control are quite simple: Make the center of gravity coincide with the center of pressure. In practice, this is quite difficult because wind and motion of the airplane continuously change the center of pressure. The Wright brothers had a simple solution to this problem: ". . . practice is the key to the secret of flying."[9] They spent hours acquiring the skills to fly a plane—not just the technology of the plane itself.[10]

The Wright brothers' triumph can teach us three critical lessons:

- Divide big problems into smaller problems.

- Focus on the smaller problems that aren't solved.

- Don't waste time and energy tinkering with problems that have already been solved.

Copy Mother Nature

Long before the Wright brothers, butterflies were taking to the air, and their wings illustrate the next principle: Copy Mother Nature.

Ioannis Miaoulis, dean of Tuft's college of engineering,* has studied the design of butterfly wings. You've probably never heard of them described in this way, but butterfly wings are multilayered thin-films made up of alternating layers of air and a material called chitin. (Chitin is the rough, protein-like material that is most recognizable as the exoskeleton of crabs, lobsters, and most insects.) One would think that with

---

*<http://www.tufts.edu/as/engdept>

these physical properties (air pockets and rough material), butterfly wings would absorb heat in an uneven manner, but Miaoulis found that butterfly wings absorb heat without "hotspots."[11]

Meanwhile the semiconductor industry is trying its best to eliminate hotspots in computer chips because uneven heating affects the performance of the chips. To accomplish this, industry experts have been trying to create smooth surfaces of uniform thickness. But from Miaoulis's work, it turns out that the way to eliminate hotspots may be to follow Mother Nature's lead and create uneven surfaces.

Nature is a research and development lab that's been perfecting real-world solutions for the past few billion years. Following nature's lead even has a name today: biomimicry. It is trying to answer questions like:

- How do chimpanzees cure themselves of ailments by eating leaves?

- How do spiders weave fibers far stronger, lighter, and more flexible than anything man has created?

- How can mussels attach themselves under conditions that leave man's best glues flapping in the wind?

Work the edges

What really matters happens at the edges—that is, where one surface or material meets or changes into another—is a key principle of architecture. The action is not in the centers or areas of sameness.[12]

This is a sound principle for revolutionaries too. The essence of Macintosh, for example, is the edge, or interaction, between the human and computer. Macintosh is very good at bridging what a person wants to do and getting a computer to do it.

If you want to change the rules, then, look for edges like these:

- **People and machine interaction.** Macintosh is my personal example, but there are many undiscovered ways that working with machines could be better.

- **People and people interaction.** E-mail, on-line chats, and videoconferencing are examples of ways interpersonal interaction has changed.

- **Company and people.** The now legendary customer service of Nordstrom changed the rules and expectations people had for a shopping experience.

- **Company and company.** Dell's* parts vendors are located in the same building as its production facilities—truly, just-in-time delivery between vendor and customer.

Stage 3: Precipitate

I call the third stage Precipitate because of a memory from chemistry class. One experiment in the lab consisted of mixing a solution of silver nitrate with a solution of sodium chloride—two liquids. Lo and behold, out fell a solid precipitate (silver chloride).

$$AgNO_3 + NaCl \rightarrow AgCl + Na^+ + NO_3^-$$

This was an "aha!" moment for me: Combining two liquids can make a solid![†]

The same type of magic moment occurs when you're thinking different: All of a sudden, out of nowhere (though we know how much background processing went on), out drops something solid. Here are some examples of great thought precipitation.

- **Physical.** Staffers at Dean Junior College[‡] (in Franklin, Massachusetts) lost potential customers who didn't have

---

* <http://www.dell.com/>

[†] As the old saying goes: If you're not a part of the solution, then you're part of the precipitate.

[‡] <http://www.dean.edu/>

time to take a course at the college, so they started "ChooChooU" on the commuter train into and out of Boston. This broke the rule of teaching classes in static locations. Students heard lectures during their commute and went to the college on the weekends to take exams.[13]

- **Temporal.** Insurance claimants in car accidents often have to wait for estimates from auto body shops, appraisals from an insurance adjuster, and paperwork processing. Boston's Plymouth Rock Assurance Corporation created a fleet of Crash Busters that has changed this process. Each Crash Buster van is equipped with a complete mini office including a computer, modem, cellular phone, laser printer, and swiveling desk chair. The claims appraiser or "Crash Buster" is dispatched to the accident scene, makes all the necessary repair appraisals, and cuts a check for the customer on the spot.[14]

EXERCISE

How long did it take you to get an insurance settlement the last time you had a car accident?

- **Geographical.** The Charlie Case Tire Company runs a car service center. By traditional rules, most car repair shops are close to people's homes or offices. Not this one—it's at the Phoenix airport. Why? So that you can drop your car off for new tires or an oil change when taking a trip out of town. The Charlie Case people take you to the airline terminal and pick you up when you return. There's no downtime for your car; you don't have to arrange for a ride; and you pay only $3.75 per day for parking.

- **Industry traditions.** One rule of most music groups is to prevent people from making bootleg recordings at concerts. Black-market recordings, most industry people believe, cannibalize sales of the group's CDs, tapes, and records. One group who defied this rule was the Grateful Dead.* They went so far as to provide an area right up front to facilitate recordings by their fans. These recordings spread the word about the Grateful Dead, led to greater concert attendance, and improved record sales as well as created a closer relationship with fans with one simple change.[15]

- **Customer needs.** Most airlines, or at least most classes of service on airlines, adhere to this rule: Cram as many people into the airplanes as possible and skimp on the food to make a profit. By contrast, Midwest Express Airlines[†] treats everyone like a first-class passenger and believes that repeat business is the key to making a profit.[16] Midwest configures its planes with four seats in each row instead of five like most other airlines. (There isn't a coach and first class; the entire plane is configured this way.) The meals are elaborate, freshly prepared, and served with wine on real china with linen napkins.

- **Rules of engagement.** Competition between rivals is usually governed by unspoken (and often inexplicable) rules of engagement. For example, in 1995 two television stations, WBTV and WSOC, in Charlotte, North Carolina, used sweepstakes to increase their ratings. Viewers watched the stations to see if their numbers were selected. Soon, the stations were trying to outdo each other by a traditional rule of engagement: Give away more money than the competition. A third station, WCNC,[‡] didn't give away any money; instead, it showed the winning numbers of both stations. Its ratings increased by 83 percent without giving away a dime![17]

- **Product definition.**[18] Amil International Health Corporation[§] is a fast-growing health care insurance company in Brazil.

---

*<http://grateful.dead.net/>

†<http://www.midwestexpress.com/>

‡<http://www.wcnc.com/>

§<http://www.amil.com.br/>

One of the primary reasons for Amil's success is that it breaks the rules of what defines (or limits) a product. Amil has its own chain of pharmacies, a twenty-four-hour-a-day doctor hotline,[19] a Health Rescue Plan where for $2 per month you are transported to a hospital in a helicopter in a medical emergency, a children's club to teach good medical habits, and free lectures for business people, with speakers like Peter Drucker.

Be Lucky (or Why Blind, Dumb Luck Is Often Not So Blind or Dumb)

I concede that many revolutionary ideas are the result of blind, dumb luck. If you're lucky, you can skip Purge, Prod, and Precipitate and go straight to being lucky. Much as we'd like to believe that invention and revolution are always the result of systematic and linear problem solving, it's not true. But there are ways to *increase* your luck.

Harness naïveté

Naïveté is empowering. Here's a story that illustrates this point—it may be apocryphal, but I never let confirmation stand in the way of a good story.

When new engineers joined the incandescent lighting group of General Electric* in the 1930s, the director of the division liked to play a joke on them. He assigned them the task of inventing a coating for light bulbs that would remove the hotspot in the then current state-of-the-art design.

The joke was that this uniform glow bulb was "impossible" to create. Engineer after engineer tried and failed at this task. When each newbie admitted failure and was told the task was impossible, the scene brought out laughter from the rest of the engineers.

This was a wonderful initiation rite until around 1952,

---

* <http://www.ge.com/>

when a new engineer brought in his creation, screwed it in, turned it on, and asked the director if this was what he was looking for. Upon seeing the "impossible bulb," the director said, "Ah, yup. That's it."[20]

In a way, this is a corollary to thinking different: "Find someone who has not yet thought about the problem at all or someone who doesn't 'know' it's impossible."

Harvest entre-manure

Entre-manure is the result of an entrepreneur stumbling into an unintended consequence (AKA, manure) that is more valuable than what he was originally looking for.[21] Take Teflon, for example. Most of us think of it as the nonstick coating for pots and pans, but the DuPont* scientist who discovered it in 1938 was hardly looking to improve life in the kitchen.

The scientist was Roy Plunkett. He was working on a project to create a new type of Freon—a chemical used as a refrigerant—that would not infringe on another company's patent. He did not intend to create a new compound for pots and pans.

When Plunkett discovered this new material, he did the right thing: He remained curious about the results and conducted more chemical tests on it. He didn't ignore what happened because it wasn't what he wanted. When he couldn't get any of the basic reagents to react with this mystery material, he concluded that his process caused polymerization (many simple molecules of one type combining one long chain).

He sent some of the material to DuPont's Central Research Department, where they noticed how slick and chemically inert the new material was. The outbreak of World War II and the project to build an atomic bomb pushed Plunkett's discovery into service. It was used in the manufacturing process of the radioactive isotope of uranium and also molded into nose cones for proximity bombs.

More than a decade after the end of the war, DuPont was

---

*<http://www.dupont.com/>

able to manufacture Teflon cheaply enough for use in consumer goods.[22] The discovery and use of Teflon teaches three lessons:

- Be curious about unintended findings.

- Establish a company atmosphere that encourages seemingly unapplied research and discovery.

- Stick with a discovery and it may yield important commercial products.

Exploit "latent potential"[23]

Latent potential is a concept of Stephen Jay Gould, the Harvard* biologist. He postulates that some structures on animals may have served one purpose and also embodied the latent potential to serve other purposes. He illustrates this concept with what he calls the "5-percent-of-a-wing-problem." That is, we can understand how a fully developed wing is a marvelous adaptive device that provides the ability to fly. But what good was 5 percent of a wing?

The answer is that 5 percent of a wing—perhaps a row of feathers—doesn't enable an organism to fly, but it does provide an excellent way to conserve heat. Thus, the precursors of wings for flying may have been feathers for thermoregulation. Early wings may well have had the function of conserving heat and the latent potential for flight.

What do a few feathers on a prehistoric bird have to do with thinking different, catalyzing a revolution, and blind, dumb luck? A great deal, actually. It means being open to and exploiting any unforeseen features of your products or services.

Consider, for example, the cigarette lighter in your car. Originally, it had probably only one purpose: Enabling you to slowly kill yourself and your passengers as you drove. Car designers didn't anticipate the widespread need for a power source for cellular phones and radar detectors. Going further, a

---

*<http://www.harvard.edu/>

A blender for your car from Whistler Corporation.

company called Whistler Corporation has created cigarette-lighter powered fans, bullhorns, coffee makers, blenders, and hair dryers. Recently, many car manufacturers have offered multiple cigarette-lighter outlets not for lighting cigarettes but for all the gizmos a family uses in a car.

Latent potential is often unintended and can exist because of luck or happenstance. But when it does occur, it is an excellent way to change the rules.

Readings for Revolutionaries*

Biomimicry—Innovation Inspired by Nature, Janna M. Benyus, William Morrow, 1997, ISBN: 0688136915.

Decision Traps—Ten Barriers to Brilliant Decision-Making and How to Overcome Them, J. Edward Russo and Paul J. H. Schoemaker, Fireside, 1990, ISBN: 0671726099.

Extraordinary Popular Delusions and the Madness of Crowds, Charles MacKay, Crown Publishers, 1995, ISBN: 051788433X.

If You Want to Write—A Book About Art, Independence and Spirit, Brenda Ueland, Graywolf Press, 1997, ISBN: 1555972608.

The Quark and the Jaguar—Adventures in the Simple and the Complex, Murray Gell-Mann, W. H. Freeman, 1994, ISBN: 0716725819.

The Structure of Scientific Revolutions, Thomas S. Kuhn, University of Chicago Press, 1996, ISBN: 0226458083.

Uncommon Genius—How Great Ideas Are Born, Denise G. Shekerjian, Penguin USA, 1991, ISBN: 0140109862.

---

*At the end of each chapter, I provide a list of required, not recommended, reading for the revolutionary. Contrary to *The Chicago Manual of Style*, I list them alphabetically according to title with the publication date of the most recent (and paperback if possible) version that I could find and the ISBN number—all of this is designed to help you buy the book with the greatest ease.

2

Don't Worry, Be Crappy

More progress results from the violent execution of an imperfect plan than the perfection of a plan to violently execute.

Hubert Humphrey

Macintosh, the Crappy Computer

In January 1984, I helped ship a crappy product. It had only 128K of RAM, no hard disk (which was fine because there was no application software), no modem, no slots, no color display, no letter-quality printer, no documentation, no installed customer base, and no development tools. It was, of course, the first version of the Macintosh personal computer.

We (that is, the Macintosh Division of Apple Computer) could have waited until Macintosh was "perfect." However, waiting would have added a year of delay and probably would have killed Macintosh because we were already burned out, the software developers who were creating applications would have lost confidence that Macintosh would ever ship, and who knows how the computer market would have changed in a year's time.

To paraphrase Bobby McFerrin, sometimes "don't worry, be crappy" and ship an imperfect product—not because you want to (or think you can) get away with it, but because it's the right thing to do.

Revolutionary products don't fail because they are shipped too early. They fail because they aren't revised fast enough. (The process of revision is the subject of the next chapter.) Truth and humility be known, most products were crappy in their first iteration—especially looking backwards.

How many times have you looked at the first version of a breakthrough product and thought, "How could they have left off such an important feature—one they had the technology to incorporate at the time?!" But when you first saw it, you and everyone else were so taken with the product and what it could do that its shortcomings were hardly noticeable.

To execute the "Don't Worry, Be Crappy" philosophy, you need great products, great teams, and great processes.

Great Products*

I wrote my first book, *The Macintosh Way*, in 1990. When I read it now, I am embarrassed by its crudeness—this kind of embarrassment often paralyzes people and prevents them from shipping in the first place. Luckily, I didn't realize it was crude because it sold 30,000 copies—"Don't worry, be happy!"

In the book, I invented the acronym DICE to describe a great product. DICE stands for Deep, Indulging, Complete, and Elegant. Now, seven years later, I'm releasing version 2.0, and I'd like to add another E, for Evocative. This makes the acronym DICEE.

Deep

Great products are deep. Their features and functions satisfy desires that you didn't know you had at the time of purchase. The mark of a deep product is wishing it had a feature after

---

*I will frequently use the term "products" to refer to both products and services.

you've used it for a while and then discovering that it already does.

Deep products grow with you, so you don't have to buy another product soon thereafter. Indeed, a savvy consumer will buy a product or service that, though too deep initially, will allow for future growth as the user becomes more sophisticated.

My favorite example of a deep product is a watch called the Breitling Aerospace.* On one level, it's merely a watch with hands and numerals, but over time you come to learn of its depth: the ability to let you tell time with analog hands or digits, see what time it is in at least two other time zones, determine how much longer an airplane flight should last, and figure out how long you've been jogging.†

Indulging

A great product or service is indulging. It is more than what you minimally need and costs more than what you could have minimally spent. Would I die if I used a watch that didn't have all the features of a Breitling Aerospace? Hardly, but I feel pampered, fortunate, and cool because I own one—I feel indulged.

The Bang and Olufsen‡ Beo Sound 9000 system is another example of an indulgent product. It is a music station with a six-CD player and an AM/FM radio. The CDs are lined up in a row, behind a tempered glass panel with a motorized door.

You can mount the player horizontally or vertically, and you can angle it up or lay it flat. The system's control panel is

---

* <http://www.breitling.com/>

† The Breitling Aerospace has one feature, however, that I cannot figure out when to use. If you press the crown, it uses four different tones to tell you what time it is. I guess you could be trapped while spelunking, unable to turn your wrist to look at the luminescent dial, but able to press down the crown with your other hand. This feature will then enable you to hear what time it is before you die.

‡ <http://www.bangsf.com/>

attached by magnets and can be adjusted to any angle as well. Your favorite radio stations and the titles and favorite tracks of up to 200 CDs are programmable into the system.

A large twelve-character LED display with a "headlight" ensures you can see the title and number of the track currently playing, along with time remaining. You can adjust the position of the display panel for optimized readability. When the CD stops spinning, the "autopositioning" feature stops it in the exact position in which it was first placed in the holder. That way, you can read the words and graphics on the CD itself.

Expensive doesn't necessarily mean indulging. Many expensive products are not indulgent—they are simply stupid—while some very inexpensive products are surprisingly indulgent. For example, the whiteness and the beautiful, smooth finish of First Choice laser paper from Weyerhauser make this paper indulgent.[1] And a $20 haircut in Tokyo involves five attendants, a full upper body massage, shaved eyebrows, four heated shampoos, and a parting gift.[2]

Complete

A complete product provides all the attributes that make it delightful. Don't confuse Complete with Deep. The Breitling Aerospace is deep, but if service for the watch was poor, it would not be complete (in fact, the service is excellent, so a Breitling is both deep and complete). Deep is the product; complete is the documentation, service, and support.

DirectTire* Sales of Watertown, Massachusetts, is an example of a complete service. The company rebalances tires and fixes flats for the life of the tires at no charge. And don't worry about getting to work when you have to leave your car for repair because there are fourteen loaner cars for customers to use.

If none of these loaners is available, or if customers prefer, DirectTire will pay for a cab service to and from the garage. While customers wait, they can use a spotless lounge and enjoy

---

*<http://www.directtire.com/>

magazines, fresh coffee, real cream, and doughnuts. For a small fee, DirectTire will store winter tires for customers and will mount, balance, and change the tires twice a year at no charge.

Elegant

The downside of a deep product is feature-itis. Without elegant design, people cannot figure out how to use deep products, and they may even come to resent them. I can access all of the Breitling Aerospace features by using only the stem—the watch is not covered with buttons like most digital watches.

A great product combines elegance with depth. Elegance, though, is the most difficult DICEE quality to explain and to implement because it is usually in the eye of the beholder. However, elegant products adhere to these principles:

- **Honor aesthetics.** Elegant products show that someone cared about what the product looked like. There is a smoothness

The deep and elegant Breitling Aerospace.

and polish that reflects the creator's pride. Elegant products aren't simply functional; they are also beautiful.

- **Indicate that form follows function.** The physical form of an elegant product follows its function. Two anti-examples: To replace two sparkplugs in a Chevrolet Monza, you had to remove the engine. To read *Wired*, you have to be a masochist because of its page design. Form, in these cases, conflicts with function.

- **Use materials truthfully.** Elegant products use materials in logical, natural ways. Materials are not used to make a statement or to jar people's sensibilities. A computer made out of teak, for example, is a dishonest use of wood.

- **Permit direct and immediate manipulation.** Elegant products enable users to control and not be controlled. Actions are concrete, not abstract, and the user, not the product, initiates control.

- **Provide constant feedback.** Elegant products let a user know what's going on: Is a process progressing? Have you hit a stumbling block? Users are not left to guess the current state of a process.

- **Show forgiveness.** Elegant products forgive mistakes. They do not allow people to trap themselves in situations that are impossible to reverse. The best example of this is the undo command in many software products.

EXERCISE

Forward a phone call to another extension in your company.

Evocative

Finally, a great product catalyzes strong feelings: People either love it or hate it, and there are few people in between. Great products are emotive for two reasons:

- **They enhance people's lives.** They make people feel more creative, productive, and happy. Thus, an emotional bond develops between great product or services and people.

- **They threaten some people's comfort level.** An innovative, superior product or service often causes turbulence in the status quo of people's thinking, and small minds hate turbulence.

This doesn't mean that when people hate your product or service, you've got a winner. And it doesn't mean that you should design a product or service that people will hate. But you should strive to create something that some people will love rather than something everyone will merely like. Believe me, if you succeed, the haters will come, but the commitment from the people who love your product will outweigh their negativity.

But I digress . . . just remember the acronym: DICEE. Deep. Indulging. Complete. Elegant. Evocative.

Great Teams

At least once in your life, I hope that you have a chance to work on a team like the Macintosh Division of Apple Computer. We were, arguably, the greatest collection of egomaniacs in Silicon Valley, and Silicon Valley is full of egomaniacs, so this is saying a lot. But we were a great team who created a revolution that changed computers forever.

These are the qualities of great teams that I learned about from working in the division. They are applicable to anyone trying to create a revolution.

Strong Leader

What is legitimate authority? Knowing what you're doing, communicating what you're doing, and expecting the team to add value to your behavior and ideas.[3]

Great leaders are paradoxical. They catalyze, rather than control, the work of their teams. They have an overarching vision for the team but are not autocratic in the realization of this vision. Their eyes are open to whatever results occur—not just planned goals, because serendipity is a great innovator.

When dealing with the rest of the company or the industry, great leaders mutate into strong-willed egomaniacs. But they have to be strong because a long list of people are going to try to grind them down: first, the rest of the company who want an evolutionary, not revolutionary, product; second, the experts who think that something cannot be done; and third, the cowards who think that no one would buy the product even if it could be done.

In short, revolutionary leaders have to care more about what they think of themselves than what the world thinks of them.

Idealistic, busy, and often uncredentialed people

Great teams are made of people who see the current state-of-the-art as a fraction of what could be. If there was a single quality that characterized the Macintosh Division team (besides arrogance), it was idealism. We *believed* we could change the world. We described our work ("mission," really) with terms like "insanely great" and "the computer for the rest of us."

If I had to describe in one word the perfect person to start a revolution, it would be "evangineer."[4] That is, a combination of evangelist (see Chapter 5, "Make Evangelists, Not Sales") and engineer: someone who wants to change the world and has the technical knowledge to do it.

When starting a revolutionary team, don't succumb to the temptation of hiring people who are underemployed or unemployed just because it's easy to recruit them. Great people are usually contributing to important projects and are quite busy, if not unavailable. Convincing them to join a team is, in fact, the first confirmation that an idea has merit.[5]

The two most important things about people on a revolutionary team are their ability and passion. Their educational level or work experience is meaningless—most of the engineers who did the ground-breaking work of the Macintosh design didn't even graduate from college.*

Finally, it's as important to repel the wrong people as it is to attract the right people. Wrong people drive out right people and not vice versa! This is how Hallmark Cards† tries to dissuade the wrong people from applying for writer positions:

> Welcome to the Writing and Editing portfolio. We're glad you're interested in Hallmark.
>
> You're either going to love or hate the next few pages. And either way is fine.
>
> Suppose you do the exercises in this portfolio, and you find them frustrating, infuriating, or boring. Then do yourself a favor. Throw this portfolio away. You've just avoided a job you'd probably hate.
>
> But if you find the exercises challenging, invigorating, and interesting, then drop this portfolio in the mail. You may have found the kind of career you'd probably love.

EXERCISE

Examine the educational and work experience background of the colleagues you consider most effective. Do they have the most impressive backgrounds?

Small, separate, and lousy

Great teams are usually small—under fifty in total head count. (There are few examples of a team made up of hundreds of people who created anything revolutionary.) Big teams aren't conducive to revolutionary products because such products require a high degree of single-mindedness, unity, and unreasonable passion.

First, great teams need to be separate from the rest of a

---

*An observation: If a person with the right credentials says something can be done, then it probably can be done. If the person says it can't be done, then probably it still can be done.

†<http://www.hallmark.com/>

company. For example, Michael Stecyk, a twenty-year veteran of Pitney Bowes Inc., managed the team that made the highly successful Pitney Bowes Personal Post Office Mailing Center. This product is designed for small offices and home offices—a market that Pitney Bowes had ignored since it was so successful serving large companies. One of the key decisions he made was to move his division thirty miles away from the plush Pitney Bowes headquarters.[6]

Physical separation is important for these reasons.

- A cross-functional team spread throughout a company won't develop into a cohesive group. The team needs a monomaniacal allegiance to the "mission from God." Such a mission may be orthogonal and, at worst, contradict the overall goals of the organization.

- Secrecy is important in order to stay ahead of the competition. The more people trampling through an area, the more likely that secrets will leak.

- The team doesn't need (or want) feedback early in the process. Frankly, initial prototypes are usually terrible. The team needs the time and space to safely muddle through mediocrity.

Second, the team should be tightly packed in a separate and lousy building with lousy furniture. Tightly packed because as MIT Sloan School of Management professor Thomas J. Allen discovered, communication between people dropped off drastically when they were more than thirty meters from each other.[7]

A lousy building and lousy furniture are necessary because suffering is good for revolutionaries. It builds cohesiveness; it creates a sense of urgency; and it focuses the team on what's most important: shipping! If you are ever recruited by a team that claims to be revolutionary and see beautiful, matched Herman Miller* furniture, run, do not walk, from the interview. On the other hand, if you see a lousy building, lousy furniture, but fantastically creative workspaces, then sign up immediately.

---

*<http://www.hermanmiller.com/>

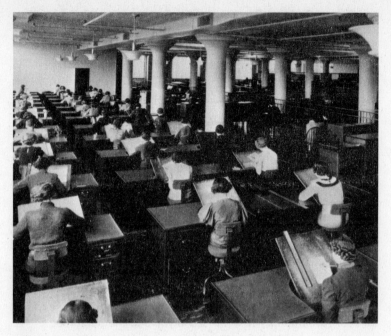

The design department of Hallmark Cards in the early days.

Circa 1998, Kelly Barnett's cubicle at Hallmark Cards. What a difference a few decades make.

Casual and unregimented atmosphere

If a team has a strong, revolutionary leader, people, and physical setting, it's very unlikely that the atmosphere would be formal and regimented. However, I'll state this outright rather than take any chances: A team of revolutionaries thrives in a casual and unregimented structure where people communicate openly, and the mission overshadows bureaucratic considerations and corporate hierarchy.

This is not to say that this type of structure is best as the revolution enters the mainstream of a company or industry, but it is certainly necessary for recruitment, product creation, and first shipment.

EXERCISE

The Shopping Center Test. When you are considering someone for your revolutionary team, pretend you see the person at a shopping center, but she has not yet spotted you. Which action do you take?

    A. Rush over and say hello.

    B. Leave bumping into her to chance.

    C. Duck into a store before she sees you.

(Members of your team should be in the first category.)

Great Practices

The final component of a revolution is great practices: How the team moves forward from an idea to a product. Here are the seven great practices that will help you move through this process.

#1 Dare to find fault with existing products and services

A good starting point for revolutionaries is to find fault with existing products and services and then do something big to improve them. The Macintosh Division was dissatisfied with the personal computers of the early 1980s.

Back then, the computers were too hard to use and expensive. They appealed to hobbyists and hackers because only hobbyists and hackers could use them. They were used by businesses and universities because only businesses and universities could afford them. If we hadn't dared to have an idealistic belief that things could, and should, be better, Macintosh would have never been created.

An important point is that revolutionaries are not always forged out of total hardship and deprivation.* As Henry Petroski says, "Luxury, rather than necessity, is the mother of invention."[8] That is, revolutionaries have the luxury of envisioning a better product, service, or world because they already have a taste of what could be.

#2 Go with your gut

Hal Sperlich had a vision: a family car more useful than a station wagon. His dream vehicle was large enough for comfortable grocery shopping and car pooling, but also featured good handling and front-wheel drive like passenger cars. At the time (the 1970s), consumers had to choose between capacity and handling.

EXERCISE

Load yourself, your spouse, your three kids, two grandparents, and two strollers in a station wagon.

When Sperlich first started developing the idea of a minivan, he met with great resistance from his superiors at Ford Motor Company.† "They lacked confidence that a market

---

*In this way, business revolutions differ radically from political revolutions.

†<http://www.ford.com/us/>

existed because the product didn't exist," recalls Sperlich. "In ten years of developing the minivan, we never once got a letter from a housewife asking us to invent one. To the skeptics, that proved there wasn't a market out there."[9]

Sperlich showed a true mark of a revolutionary: relying on intuition and feel and believing so much in his product that he got fired. "Henry Ford just didn't want to do it. Hal used to take him on, and when you do that with people around . . ." said Lee Iacocca, who was an executive at Ford at the time. In fact, Henry Ford made Iacocca fire Sperlich.[10]

Out of Ford, Sperlich joined Iacocca at Chrysler* and created the minivan for his new employer. Chrysler introduced the minivan in 1983 and sold as many as half a million vehicles per year—cornering a market that Japanese competitors had never even considered. Ironically, General Motors had a minivan design and the market research that supported the customer demand for it, but the idea was killed because of a lack of resources,[11] guts, or vision.

The lesson: Use your intuition to create a revolutionary product. People are notoriously poor at articulating anything besides improvements to the products they currently own. Market research is a pathetic catalyst for revolutionary products. Oxymoronic as this may seem, sometimes you have to "hear" what people would say if only they knew better.

To wit, Chrysler built a minivan that no housewives asked for, and no one asked for a cute little computer that smiled at you when you turned it on, used something called a mouse to control it, and had icons on the screen rather than text. Everyone was asking for a faster MS-DOS computer.

#3 Design for yourself

It all started when my daughters were young, and I took them to amusement parks on Sunday. I sat on a bench

---

* <http://www.chrysler.com/>

eating peanuts and looking all around me. I said to myself, dammit, why can't there be a better place to take your children, where you can have fun together?

Walt Disney[12]

Why was the dishwasher invented? You probably think it was invented because people wanted to save time by loading it up, starting it, and moving on to other activities. Guess again.

Josephine Cochrane, the wife of an Illinois politician, invented the dishwasher in 1886. She was wealthy and had many servants, so saving time and effort wasn't the issue. Rather, her servants were breaking too many dishes doing them manually, so she invented it for her own needs.

She received many orders from hotels and restaurants because her dishwasher saved labor and broke fewer dishes. However, she ran into an interesting problem: Homeowners did not consider dishwashing an onerous task, so she had to sell the dishwasher on the basis of providing a more sterile wash because of hotter water.[13]

When all else fails, go back to the most basic rule of product development: Design what you would like to use. At least you know there's one customer for your product. This is more than most market researchers can identify.

#4 Shake and bake

When Jim Manzi took over Industry.net, the world was going to be his oyster. As the former CEO of Lotus Development Corporation,* he had the pedigree to be the revolutionary to collect fees on the thousands of on-line sales transactions. All the ingredients were there: world-class entrepreneur and red-hot market (Internet transactions).[14]

He renamed the company Nets Inc. and moved it from Pittsburgh to beautiful offices in Cambridge, Massachusetts.

---

*<http://www.lotus.com/>

He hired executives from Lotus and built an infrastructure of sixty engineers to manage the software and hardware that would support a huge volume. He even merged the company with giant AT&T's organization called New Media Services.

In May 1997, unfortunately, Nets Inc. declared bankruptcy. The burn rate of the company around that time was $1 million per month, but its sales volume could not support the infrastructure costs. Perhaps Manzi was too early. Perhaps his plans were too grandiose. He should have shaked and baked instead:

Throw some simple and cheap ingredients in a bag, shake it, bake it, and go to market.

In other words, build a prototype and get on with it.

Kagi Shareware* did just that. This Berkeley, California–based company represents over 1,200 shareware programmers and their 3,400 software products. The company started as the hobby of Kee Nethery; as the business grew, Nethery recruited his wife, son, and friends. The company started out by using simple and cheap software (HyperCard and Eudora) running on simple and cheap computers (a Macintosh IIci and Macintosh Classic) to create an Internet payment processing system.

The first office was Nethery's bedroom. His computer equipment was on a desk in the bedroom, so when his wife wanted to go to bed, he had to roll his chair out of the way so she could get past him. He estimates that the size of Kagi's first "office" was four square feet. He had to take a second computer out of the bedroom because its fan was too loud and disturbed the couple's sleep.

Kagi Shareware is an example of a company that bootstrapped itself and became a success without truckloads of capital. Taken together, Nets Inc. and Kagi Shareware illustrate that too much money is worse than too little. As Nethery says, "Companies with too much funding and not enough real world experience tend to solve imaginary problems."

---

*<http://www.kagi.com/>

#5 Get on base and leave home runs to chance

Kagi Shareware illustrates another great practice: Concentrate on getting on base and let home runs happen. Nets Inc. swung for the fence by building an infrastructure of people, computers, and software, whereas Kagi just tried to survive and build a business.

It's not your money, so why not go for the home run? Call me a romantic, but you should never squander money, whether it's yours or someone else's. Initially Kagi may have only hit a single, but once it got on base it had the opportunity to score. Nets Inc. is out of the game.

Indeed, most home runs in business started out as mere singles, then good fortune and timing took over. Any baseball manager will tell you that his ideal team is filled with solid hitters, not homerun sluggers.

For example, in 1886 Richard Sears hit a single by selling a shipment of watches that was refused by a jeweler in North Redwood, Minnesota.[15] At the time, Sears was working for a railroad station agent and had become familiar with the pricing of various merchandise from their bills of lading.

Sears bought the watches for $12 each, sold them to other station agents for $14 each, and let them keep whatever profits they made. Over the first six months, Sears made $5,000.[16] From this single, he discovered the profit-through-volume strategy that became the home run called Sears.

#6 Ignore naysayers

The defenders of the status quo will almost always tell you that your idea won't work or that it's not necessary. After all, they built the status quo, and you are now attacking them! Thus, ignoring naysayers is necessary to create a revolution. Here is a list of the major categories of people to ignore and why.

Naysayer #1: Customers and market research

As a medium there is so much cross-talk and opinion-influencing that unless that is exactly what you are try-

ing to get pegged, they [focus groups] are too dangerous
for human consumption.

Geoffrey Moore

Customers and market research affirm bad things (New
Coke, for example) and trash good things. Asking customers
open-ended questions like, "What would you want?" or
"Would you use . . . ?" guarantees average-ness. People vote
for the commonplace and the familiar rather than the breakthrough because it's more comfortable to do so.

Even though surveys showed that there was no need for
another network, media mogul Barry Diller went ahead and created Fox Broadcasting.* Diller spoke on the subject to *Fortune*,
saying, "We've become slaves to demographics, to market
research, to focus groups. We produce what the numbers tell us to
produce. And gradually, in this dizzying chase, our senses lose
feeling and our instincts dim, corroded with safe action."[17]

Imagine what customers would have told Polaroid† about a
new-fangled camera that was thirty times more costly than the
Kodak Baby Brownie.[18] Or what they would have told FedEx‡
about a method of shipping that was one hundred and fifty
times more expensive than a stamp.[19]

Naysayer #2: Critics and schmexperts§

Charles Kettering, the legendary inventor who worked for
General Motors,‖ put it best:

If I want to stop a research program, I can always do it
by getting a few experts to sit in on the subject, because

---

*<http://www.fox.com/>

†<http://www.polaroid.com/>

‡<http://www.fedex.com/>

§If you can't figure out the definition of *schmexpert*, you probably
shouldn't be reading this book.

‖<http://www.generalmotors.com/>

they know right away that it was a fool thing to try in the first place.[20]

In a classic schmexpert's blunder, IBM* turned down the sales rights to the paper copier that would become the Xerox copier. In 1959, when Haloid made the offer, IBM hired a major consulting firm to advise them. After three months of research, the firm advised IBM not to acquire the technology because they estimated the worldwide potential for a plain-paper copier to be less than 5,000 units.[21]

Unfortunately, Xerox† itself fell prey to schmexperts, too. They did not enter the small copier business on advice from consultants. Instead, Japanese manufacturers came along to miniaturize the copier, leaving Xerox with a 50 percent decline in market share.

People don't just condemn only other people's inventions, they sometimes underestimate their own:

> The talking motion picture will not supplant the regular silent motion picture. . . . [T]here is such a tremendous investment to pantomime pictures that it would be absurd to disturb it.[22]
>
> *Thomas Alva Edison, at the first public demonstration of his talking picture machine, 1913*

Naysayer #3: Your own company

Revolutionaries who work within an ongoing company will attest to the fact that it's (ironically) often necessary to ignore your own colleagues. Here are three typical examples.

- **Engineering.** Many an opportunity has been lost because engineering fell in love with a technology and wanted to

---

*<http://www.ibm.com/>

†<http://www.xerox.com/>

produce "the perfect product." Sometimes you have to ignore the engineers who want to add a few more features, or a competitor will seize control of the market.

- **Sales force.** A company's sales force typically has the short-term outlook of meeting this quarter's quota. They will usually reinforce the customers' requests to evolve current products and to sell them more cheaply.

- **Management.** The higher you go in a company, the less oxygen there is, so supporting intelligent life becomes difficult. Thus, you may have to ignore the people high within the hierarchy who only have the brainpower to comprehend the status quo.

Here's an inspiring example of ignoring your own management: Werner Forssman pioneered human cardiac catheterization in 1929.[23] According to *Medicine,* this was Forssman's course of action:

> Ignoring his department chief, and tying his assistant to an operating table to prevent her interference, he placed a urethral catheter into a vein in his own arm, advanced it to the right atrium, and walked upstairs to the x-ray department where he took the confirmatory x-ray.[24]

Naysayer #4: The competition

> When the focus of attention is on ways to beat the competition, strategy inevitably gets defined primarily in terms of the competition.[25]
>
> *Kenichi Ohmae,* The Borderless World

This is a tricky recommendation: Revolutionaries should watch their competition but not necessarily assume they know what they're doing and emulate them. (One of the most interesting things people learn when they go to work for a competitor is how messed up the new employer is.)

Yamaha* ignored the competition when it made a digital piano while the competition was making only traditional pianos or synthesizers. A traditional piano didn't have the flexibility of music synthesis. A synthesizer was flexible, but it was too ugly to put in a living room.

Yamaha ignored the conventional wisdom of its competition and added the capabilities of a synthesizer to a traditional piano. By doing this, Yamaha expanded its market to people who wanted the best of both the digital and analog worlds and leaped ahead of other piano manufacturers who were still focusing on making variations of traditional pianos.[26]

#7 Go with your "guts"

"Go with your gut," explained earlier with the Chrysler minivan example, refers to using your intuition to create something when no one is asking for it. It is the visceral reaction to an idea.

A practice that sounds similar (but isn't) is to go with your guts—having the courage to commit to a product or service once you've gone with your intuition to create it.

For example, Corning† built a factory to manufacture optical fiber before there was any market for it.[27] "We were certain this would be a product people would use," says Don Keck, the inventor of the first low-loss optical fiber. "We had a vision that optical fiber would eventually replace copper networks."

In 1982, after the U.S. deregulation of the telecommunications industry, MCI was born and gave Corning its first order. Today optical fiber is replacing copper cables throughout long-distance telephone networks and cable TV, and many utilities are using fiber optics to monitor and locate breakdowns in their plants and networks.

Nota bene: Swashbuckling entrepreneurship aside, going with your guts is a very risky practice. It helps, as in Corning's case, to be part of an ongoing corporation that can take huge

---

*<http://www.yamaha.com/>

†<http://www.corning.com/>

risks. However, an ongoing corporation is unlikely to have the courage to take a risk. A young, single-product company usually has to be more cautious—see "Shake and Bake" above.

The Order of Magnitude Test

Now that you understand creating a great product with great people and great practices, the final issue is, "When do we stop worrying about being crappy and start shipping?"

Two answers, albeit smart-ass ones, are, "When you run out of money," or "When your venture capitalists tell you to." Hopefully, these two conditions are not what are prompting you to ship. And if they are, the situation might be out of control anyway.

Instead, use the order of magnitude test: Your product or service is ready to ship when it promises a commanding new value proposition that pushes the state of the market to the next curve. Ten percent, 50 percent, or even 500 percent better than the status quo is not enough. Your revolution has to be at least 1,000 percent—ten times—or an "order of magnitude" improvement.

The best way to see if you have achieved order of magnitude improvement is to compare your product to historical examples. Ask yourself and your fellow employees if your new product or service is as much of a leap as:

OLD	NEW
Banana leaves	Plastic bags
Slide rules	Calculators
Daisy wheel printers	Laser printers
MS-DOS	Macintosh
Caterpiller	Butterfly
Crumbled leaves	Toilet paper

EXERCISE

Buy a book of ledger paper at your bookstore. Ask your accounting staff to "run some numbers" using it.[28]

A second way to determine if you've passed the order of magnitude test is to see if you and your colleagues have come to depend on the new product or service for your own success.[29] Long before Macintosh was shipped, we were addicted to using it in our day-to-day work (for example, writing marketing plans) in the Macintosh Division. This isn't just "eating your own dog food" but *loving* your own dog food and not wanting to eat anything but your own dog food.

When your product or service passes these hurdles, you will find that the revolutionary gains so outweigh the minor and temporary crappiness that shipping is a moral obligation.

Readings for Revolutionaries

The Design of Everyday Things, Donald A. Norman, Doubleday, 1990, ISBN: 0385267746.

The Evolution of Useful Things, Henry Petroski, Vintage Books, 1994, ISBN: 0679740392.

Marketing High Technology—An Insider's View, William H. Davidow, Free Press, 1986, ISBN: 002907990X.

The Power of Product Platforms—Building Value and Cost Leadership, Marc H. Meyer and Alvin P. Lehnerd, Free Press, 1997, ISBN: 0684825805.

Skunk Works—A Personal Memoir of My Years at Lockheed, Ben R. Rich and Leo Janos, Little Brown, 1996, ISBN: 0316743003.

To Engineer Is Human—The Role of Failure in Successful Design, Henry Petroski, Vintage Books, 1992, ISBN: 0679734163.

3

Churn, Baby, Churn

To improve is to change; to be perfect is to change
often.

Winston Churchill

Better . . . Better Be Coming

In the last chapter I said, "Don't worry, be crappy," but this
doesn't mean you should *stay* crappy. Instead, listen to what
your early adopters say about your revolutionary product* and
improve it accordingly because while better is the enemy of
good enough, better . . . better be coming.

I learned this lesson the first time in 1985, the year after we
introduced Macintosh. In 1984 we sold approximately 250,000
Macintoshes, but by 1985 it was clear that the market of nerds,
geeks, and dweebs who buy anything was running out. It was
time to churn the mighty Macintosh and address some of its
obvious shortcomings. But we didn't for four reasons:

- We did not want to face the fact that our baby was less than
  perfect. It was easier, albeit a stupid notion, to believe that

---

*It may seem like I'm contradicting myself here since I also told you to
ignore market research. That was for the creation of a new product,
however, not its improvement.

the market just didn't get it. We thought we were flying, but as Woody said in *Toy Story*, "That wasn't flying. That was falling with style."

- We were burned out. Many members of the Macintosh Division had spent years working under tremendous pressure for seventy hours a week (and loving it, we thought). We were exhausted.

- We found out that revising the revolution wouldn't be nearly as fun as creating it. Each incremental fix—color, slots, development tools, and debugging—was important but not nearly as sexy as shipping the first version of the product.

- We were young, immature, and naïve. Although these qualities enabled us to take on the status quo of MS-DOS, we had yet to learn that how fast you are moving is more important than where you are.

By contrast, our nemesis, Microsoft* (where quality is job 1.1[1]) is excellent at churning. Windows started out far behind, but it moved faster. As a friend once told me, "He who hesitates is DOS."[2]

VERSION	DATE OF PRESS RELEASE	FUNCTIONALITY
No version number provided.	June 28, 1985	"Microsoft Windows is an extension to the MS-DOS operating system..."[†]
No version number provided.	November 20, 1985	640K barrier broken via application swapping.
1.03	August 29, 1986	Additional device drivers, AT&T 6300 computers, and MS-DOS 3.2 support.

*<http://www.microsoft.com/>
[†]Microsoft press release, June 28, 1985

VERSION	DATE OF PRESS RELEASE	FUNCTIONALITY
2.0	April 2, 1987	Overlapping windows; new visual appearance compatible with Microsoft Operating System/2 Windows presentation manager
Windows/386	September 23, 1987	Multi-tasking of multiple MS-DOS applications; use expanded memory without additional expanded memory hardware; copying and pasting between open applications.
2.0	December 9, 1987	Two to four times speed improvement; expanded memory support; enhanced data exchange for MS-DOS applications.
3.0	May 22, 1990	Proportionally spaced system font; 3-D scroll bars and command buttons; colorful icons; user shell to shield customers from MS-DOS commands; customized desktop; user creatable screen backgrounds; user definable screen colors; use up to 16 MB of memory; desktop accessories.

VERSION	DATE OF PRESS RELEASE	FUNCTIONALITY
3.1	April 6, 1992	Context sensitive help in dialog boxes; user definable selection of the startup application; Object Linking and Embedding (OLE) for applications to work together better; improved network support; dynamic downloading of fonts and a universal printer driver.
Windows NT	May 24, 1993	Operating system for client-server computing.
Windows for Workgroups 3.11	November 8, 1993	Improved support for Novell NetWare and Windows NT.
Windows NT Server 3.5	September 13, 1994	Increased speed, reduced size, and great connectivity.
Windows NT Server 3.51	June 12, 1995	Support for PowerPC chips; improved network administration tools; support for Windows 95 Common Controls and Dialogs.
Windows 95	August 24, 1995	According to Bill Gates: "Windows 95 is about unlocking more potential of computing....It makes computing easier and more fun, and will empower people and businesses to do more with computers than has previously been possible."*

*Microsoft press release, August 24, 1995

Plan for It

Theoretically, revolutionaries should perfect a prototype of a product before it ever ships, but in the real world two things get in the way:

- First, many problems are impossible to identify beforehand. You can do a focus group, but focus groups are clean, and the real world is messy. Participants project how they would use a product—sitting comfortably in a room with other people listening to them, with conversation facilitated by a professional, and feeling like they have to express an opinion since they've been paid to be in the group. Testing begins when people have to spend their own money, and their kids throw your product down the stairs and leave it in the rain, and the dog pees on it.

- Second, employees have to see (or experience themselves) the pain that a product or service causes before they will do something about it. Hearing negative comments from focus groups and early customer testing doesn't carry enough weight to catalyze action because employees are prone to denigrate anything negative (AKA "denial"). And you can't blame them because most revolutionary products and services are not initially welcomed. But the customers' pain becomes real when you ship, and that's when the churning really begins.

To churn, you have to face the facts: The first permutation of your product isn't going to be perfect. This is a major stumbling block for young, idealistic revolutionaries. To be ready to churn as soon as the market demands it, you need to remember the first lesson of churning: "Plan for it."

Not planning for it and believing that your product is perfect or that your customers are so stupid that they will buy anything is an American perspective. One of the top managers at a Sony research facility once diagrammed his impression of American business; it was a linear model:[3]

The American Way

Concept → Engineering → Marketing → Customer

Dream up a concept, let engineering figure out how to make it, let marketing figure out how to sell it, and get it into the hands of consumers.

For their Japanese model, he drew a circle:

The Japanese Way

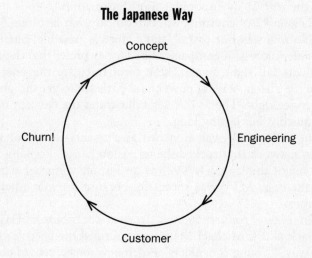

Begin with the idea, move it through engineering and production, get it to the consumer who generates feedback, modify the product, send it back to the consumer, and repeat the cycle.

Churning is the Japanese model—although one could argue that it is the Japanese model based on learning from an American named W. Edwards Deming. It means constantly revising the product with two goals in mind: making customers happy and staying ahead of the competition.

EXERCISE

Ask your employees to diagram your product development process.

Fail Quickly, But Last Long

Disneyland was a catastrophe on its opening day in 1955. The rides didn't work; there weren't enough drinking fountains; and ladies' high-heeled shoes got stuck in the still-soft asphalt. Undaunted, Walt went to work and fixed everything, until he had the world's most popular tourist attraction.[4]

Lesson #2 of churning is, "Fail quickly, but last long."

No one sets out to fail, but failure is possible. Since it is possible, successful companies like Disney prefer that their new products fail right away. These companies are the ones who have the vision, staying power, and patience to get the product or service right. The MTV* saga illustrates the concept of failing quickly, but lasting long.

In 1981 MTV was launched as a twenty-four-hour music video network that rocked the television world. Looking back, you might think that MTV was an instant winner, but this is not the case. MTV was successful because it made quick corrections.

In New Product Success Stories, contributors David J. Benjack and J. Michael MacKeen described the need for MTV this way: "Young consumers needed new music, record companies needed to recover from the post-disco sales slump, and cable companies needed to revitalize their programming."[5]

Along the way to success, MTV's ability to adapt and reinvent programming and business strategies to the ever-changing marketplace illustrates the importance of analyzing the implications of what you're doing and making corrections. Here are some of the changes MTV made:

---

* <http://www.mtv.com/>

- When MTV was first launched, founder Robert Pittman felt "the show was too much like regular television and lacked the enthusiasm and irreverence associated with rock and roll." So the talk-show style studio was revamped to look more like a teenager's garage, laden with rock memorabilia.

- The shows hosts, called "veejays," were also modified in the early years. Instead of simply announcing upcoming songs, they developed their own "personalities," each playing a certain style of music and attracting a certain following. In addition, using talent and ideas from the radio industry meant MTV was not entrenched in traditional television production values. The network's avant-garde style attracted top Hollywood directors for many music videos.

- As part of its focus on mostly suburban, white audiences, MTV did not originally play videos by black artists, and kept a strict "rock 'n' roll" format. However, in 1983 it faced legal charges for not playing Michael Jackson's *Beat It*, so MTV arranged to premiere Jackson's *Thriller* video, and began expanding its format to include black artists and other music markets.

- Pittman decided to segment the market and create a channel aimed at the older viewer, the "thirty-somethings." In 1984, Pittman bought out Ted Turner's failed music video channel and created VH1. This move ensured MTV would capture this market before a new competitor had the chance, and expanded their overall market share.

- MTV started offering theme programs catering to different market segments: *Yo! MTV Raps* for rap music, *Club MTV* for dance music, and *MTV: Unplugged* for pop and rock musicians playing acoustic versions of their music. Later innovations included a news segment, a game show called *Remote Control*, and the brazen series *Beavis and Butthead*.

EXERCISE

Pull out your old press releases, marketing plans, or engineering specifications and compare them to what you're currently shipping. How much has your product changed?

Eat Your Own Dog Food

Porsche* engineers drive on a narrow country lane to Weissach, the location of Porsche's development center. The road has uneven pavement and many dips and bends and has become Porsche's unofficial, real-world test track. When the local government planned to improve the road, Porsche's engineers convinced officials not to do this.[6] Consciously or not, they understood the third lesson of churning: "Eat your own dog food."

Eating your own dog food—using your own products—is probably the best way to reinforce the urgency of churning. Kelly Johnson, the leader of Lockheed's legendary Skunk Works,[†] once explained why he flew with test pilots in experimental aircraft:

> I figured I needed to have hell scared out of me once a year in order to keep a proper balance and viewpoint on designing new aircraft.[7]

Johnson should know about revolutionary products because the Skunk Works has produced innovative aircraft for fifty years, including the U–2, SR–71, F–117A, and YF–22. Below are four examples of companies whose employees—in some cases the executives!—eat their own dog food and stay healthier because of it.

---

*<http://www.porsche.com/>

†<http://www.lmsw.external.lmco.com/lmsw/html/index.html>

Some of the revolutionary planes that Skunk Works created.

EXERCISE

Access your Web site via a 28.8K modem.

Extra credit: Access your Web site via America Online and a 28.8K modem.

Life Sciences Corporation. Life Sciences Corporation of Rockville,* Maryland, operates Breath Alcohol Ignition Interlock Device (BAIID) programs for state governments. When repeat drunk-driving offenders are about to have their driver's licenses suspended, they are given the option to keep their license, but have an ignition and lock device installed in their cars. This device stops an individual with a breath alcohol content greater than allowed by court from driving the vehicle.

---

*<http://www.thermo.com/index.html>

The interlock devices are intrusive: They must be used not only to start the car but at random intervals during operation. Nevertheless, to encourage compliance, the interlocks have to be as user-friendly as possible without compromising their purpose.

Despite the inherent inconvenience and stigma associated with these devices, Life Sciences' president, vice president of operations, and chairman of the board had units installed in their cars. "We did it to get feedback on the unit and a second source of information on how well the unit operates," says president Michael Haines. "We also used the device to demonstrate it to other people."[8]

Gillette. Gillette* encourages its employees to use the latest in shaving technology at the company's Shaving Lab. Three hundred employees per day report unshaven to the lab to use shaving products from competitors as well as Gillette products. Employees are not given any incentives, financial or otherwise, to participate. "There's a real pride factor at Gillette," said Eric Kraus, director of communications at Gillette, "which compels employees to join in the program."

Once employees are done shaving, they answer questions regarding quality and performance using a touchpad installed in each shaving cubicle. Those who try the competition's latest shavers answer a separate set of questions. This employee feedback is passed directly to the shaving technology department.

"The Shaving Lab is an integral part of product development," says Kraus. "The Shaving Lab gives us instant feedback from some of the most critical people—Gillette employees. They want products that succeed. They'll give you the best most honest, accurate information because they're knowledgeable."[9]

Cannondale Corporation. Cannondale Corporation† of Georgetown, Connecticut, is the market leader in racing bicycles and accessories. Employees are encouraged to commute to

---

*http://www.gillette.com/>

†<http://www.cannondale.com/>

Gillette's Shaving Lab, where employees test the company's products on themselves.

work on Cannondale bicycles and to use Cannondale accessories. All employees receive 45 percent off bikes and 60 percent off clothing and accessories.

For those who want to take a quick ride during work but don't own a Cannondale bike, several company-owned bikes and prototype models are available at company headquarters. "Just come see our hallways and you'll know people are riding their bikes to work," says marketing services coordinator Diane McBergin.

The most serious riders are given free clothing and accessories to evaluate for the product development team. Of Cannondale's sixty-five employees, about a third are involved in testing products and taking their feedback to the product manager and R&D team. McBergin continues, "We depend on the people we work with as focus groups for the product development team."

Other than an occasional free article of clothing or accessory, these testers are not given any financial incentive to participate. It's simply a "part of our culture," says McBergin, who points out that these employees are already biking enthusiasts.

The Brita Products Company.* The Brita Products Company, the maker of point-of-use water filtration pitchers that remove lead, chlorine taste and color, and copper water hardness from everyday drinking water, gives employees a sample to use at home. This helps employees who take calls from customers to explain the benefits of Brita's water filters to would-be buyers. (Contrast this to the hollow pitch of telemarketers reading from a script.)

Buyers at major retailers that sell Brita products are also given free Brita samples and asked to use the product at home. Before the stores open, Brita salespeople also train many major retailers in selling and handling the filters. "If they are convinced, they will convince their customers," says CEO Heinz Hankammer.[10] In addition, Brita filters are made available at a major discount to all sales employees at these retail stores.

Starbucks coffee shops also use Brita products. This has the psychological effect of making people think that the reason Starbucks coffee tastes so good is that they use the Brita product. I doubt that Brita is donating them to Starbucks, but it would be brilliant marketing if it did.

EXERCISE

Let's fantasize about other organizations eating their own dog food. Imagine if these practices were put into place:

A. Members of Congress were required to fill out their own tax returns.

B. Airline company executives ate the same food that passengers ate in planes.[11]

C. State governors had to register their own cars at the department of motor vehicles.

D. Computer executives updated their own software.

---

*<http://www.brita.com/>

Incorporate the Means to Revise and Enhance

Lesson #4 of churning is: "Build in the means to fix your product." In the computer business, this concept is called an "open system." Computers that are "open" allow people to fix and enhance their operation in many ways:

- Adding special graphics cards or accelerator cards to beef up the hardware capabilities of the system.

- Using application software developed by companies other than the manufacturer of the computer.

- Customizing the operating system of the computer with a scripting language such as AppleScript.

- Adding peripherals such as an Iomega Jaz cartridge into the chassis of the computer to increase storage capacity.

But enough geek talk. Suppose your product is literally inside your customers, so upgrading or revising it can be a costly and dangerous process. Pacemakers are such a product. They are tiny electrical devices connected to the heart that provide voltage pulses to force the heart to beat.

Sulzer Intermedics Inc.* of Angleton, Texas, is a pioneer in software-based pacemakers. Using a device called a programmer wand, physicians can communicate with and reprogram a pacemaker while it is inside the patient.

Sulzer's pacemakers also include a device with extra memory so that technicians can temporarily add new features to the pacemaker as the company develops them. With FDA support and a patient's approval, they install and test these new features while the pacemaker is fully functioning inside the patient's body. This also allows Intermedics to correct mistakes in the pacemaker itself if an error occurred during manufacturing.

---

*<http://www.imed.com/>

Build In "Redundancy"

Another Stephen Jay Gould contribution to management theory is his concept of redundancy. By this he means that animals often have more than one structure that serves the same purpose.

For example, early fish could breathe through gills and lungs. Because their lungs were "extra," over time fish could "innovate," and their lungs became air bladders to regulate buoyancy—a development made possible because of redundancy.[12]

Like the means to revise and enhance, you can incorporate redundancy in advance if you understand the advantage of "overkill." Here's a humanitarian example. Redundant stocks of food and medical supplies in Europe gave the United States the ability to provide aid to the Soviet Union in 1992. The effort, called Operation Provide Hope, involved sending planes and trains full of supplies to relief agencies and hospitals.

Thus, redundant reserves were able to accomplish an unexpected mission in the national interest for which they had not been constituted.[13]

Document Everything

Lesson #4a of churning is: "Write down the engineering specifications of your product, so that other folks can figure out how to extend and enhance your product."

This is another lesson from the computer business. In addition to building in the means to revise and enhance a product, you also need to document the process—going well beyond how to use a product to explaining the nuts and bolts of the technology of a product. Apple, for example, published a book called *Inside Macintosh* for hardware and software developers.

This practice, however, isn't restricted to computer companies. Some car manufacturers like General Motors and Chrysler have shop manuals that are complete instructions for assembling and disassembling the entire car. These manuals make it much easier for customizers and do-it-yourselfers to work on the cars.

When you build in the means to enhance and revise a product, go all the way by writing documentation that helps your partners. Indeed, the optimal perspective is that documentation is part of the product itself, not an add-on.

Churn for Buyers, Not Nonbuyers

The knee-jerk reaction of many people is to churn a product or service to meet the objections of people who aren't buying it. For example, in Apple's case, we thought that Lotus 1–2–3 would be the magic bullet that would propel Macintosh to success in large businesses. It had no impact whatsoever.

Lesson #5 of churning: Improve your product for people who are buying it, not people who aren't.

This requires thinking different in a big way. Two kinds of customers are already buying your product: those who are using it as you intended and those who aren't. For the first group, find out what makes them happy about your product and do more of it. Plus, find out what makes them unhappy about your product and fix it.

The other kind of customer is using your product in ways you didn't plan. The users are probably not the type of customer you were trying to reach in the first place, but for some reason they find your product useful. In this case, find out what they're doing with your product and promote it because they are helping you develop a new market. Two stories illustrate this concept.

First, in the 1930s, food broker Sam Hornstein created a dog food called Balto (named after a Huskie who braved a blizzard to deliver a diphtheria serum to ill patients in Nome, Alaska). Although Hornstein was selling 50,000 cases a year, he started getting complaints because the dog food had a fishy smell. Customers said that Balto's fish products were too rich for an average dog's diet.

Rather than revising the formula to satisfy dog owners, Hornstein realized that he had another customer: cat owners. Cats were attracted to the food's fishy odor and had been eating Balto for a year. Hornstein revamped the product to cater to cats and renamed the product "Puss'N Boots." Later he sold his successful cat-food company to Quaker Oats* for $6 million.[14]

Second, Arm & Hammer† originally sold its baking soda product as a leavening product for baked goods, but a decline in recent years in home-baking reduced demand. Once people discovered it absorbed odors, they started using it as a deodorizer in refrigerators, carpets, laundry, and litter boxes. People also used it as a mild cleanser for countertops and sink drains and for brushing teeth. Because it's digestible, people take baking soda as an antacid and apply it to skin as a soothing lotion for skin irritations and tired feet.

Seeing these discoveries, Arm & Hammer changed its strategy from positioning the product as a baking ingredient to a "natural" cleanser and deodorizer. Although many customers still buy the product for baking, the growth market is for these new uses. According to author Jagdish Sheth in *Winning Back Your Market*, "A household that follows the shelf-refrigerator-drain cycle probably uses twenty times as much baking soda—same product, same package—as it would for baking purposes."[15]

Don't Hide Mistakes

Tom's of Maine,‡ the makers of natural hygiene products such as toothpaste and deodorant, was doubling sales every three years until it hit a bump with its Honeysuckle deodorant product. Tom's of Maine's actions and its customers' reactions illustrate the next lesson.

Lesson #6 of churning: "Don't try§ to hide your mistakes."

With an eye on the environment, Tom's of Maine had a goal to use less petroleum in its products. So when it was improving

---

*<http://www.QuakerOats.com/>

†<http://www.armhammer.com/>

‡<http://www.toms-of-maine.com/>

§And "try" is the operative word.

its Honeysuckle deodorant product, it replaced a petroleum derivative in the product with a vegetable-based glycerin. It also added natural antimicrobials to increase the product's odor-eating power (bacteria is the real cause of body odor).

However, two months after it introduced the new deodorant, complaints from customers started rolling in. Many said the deodorant stopped working halfway through the day. Consumer tests and the ever-increasing complaints proved that 50 percent of its customers were unhappy with the product. The company tried adding more natural antimicrobials to the product, but that still did not appease customers.

Marketing and sales staffers were demoralized, and customers were annoying stores with complaints. The company went back to the lab for a second time and replaced the natural glycerin with the original petroleum-based ingredient. "We sent samples to 200 of our angriest customers, and they loved it," said co-founder and president Tom Chappell.

Marketing and sales management suggested a total recall of the weak deodorant, but this would cost $400,000, 30 percent of the company's projected profits for the entire year. "If we were to admit failure, we'd have to rein in plans in the works to crank up our successful venture," recalls Chappell. Although painful, Chappell authorized the recall and asked managers to slow down their plans for growth and cut marketing budgets to maintain decent profits.

The company responded to all 2,000 customers who had complained. It sent a letter of explanation and apology and a free sample of the revised deodorant. "Ninety-eight percent liked it and expressed their appreciation both for the new deodorant and for how the company had handled itself," says Chappell. "Someone was listening."

Ultimately Tom's of Maine won back the trust of its customers, kept profits healthy enough for investors and shareholders, and minimized the loss of customers. It also helped the homeless to boot: Stuck with a huge amount of unused inventory, the company donated the stock of original deodorant to a company that trains homeless people in personal hygiene habits.[16]

PART 2

CREATE LIKE A GOD.

COMMAND LIKE A KING.

WORK LIKE A SLAVE.

4

Break Down the Barriers

Not choice
But habit rules the unreflecting herd.

William Wordsworth

Mazel Tov

You've shipped. Initial sales are good. You're probably extrapolating your early success, in the words of Buzz Lightyear, "To infinity and beyond." As the Japanese say, *Mazel tov*. Now get ready to fall into The Chasm.

Credit Geoffrey Moore* for this concept. He explained it in one of the best high-technology marketing books that's ever been written, *Crossing the Chasm*. Moore describes the chasm in this way:

A significant gulf, the "chasm," exists between the market made up of early adopters, and the markets of more pragmatic buyers.[1]

Early buyers are completely different from other buyers, so crossing the chasm requires breaking down the barriers that prevent widespread trial and then dominating niche markets where your products have attained success. If you dominate

---

*<http://www.chasmgroup.com/>

enough niche markets, your product will achieve critical mass and become a "no brainer" to buy.

Your product may be so compelling that early adopters beat down barriers to use it. However, the work you do to remove those barriers will make crossing the chasm easier, faster, and more likely. Indeed, if early adopters do the heavy removing, you may get a false picture of the acceptability and attractiveness of your product. This will create cata-chasmic problems in the future.

I learned this when I was president of a software company called ACIUS* which published a high-end relational database called 4th Dimension. It was so powerful and programmable that early adopters who were technically savvy flocked to it. Based on early results, we were convinced we had a hit on our hands. We fell in the chasm, though, because 4th Dimension was too hard to use for most people.

Types of Barriers

> Build up, build up, prepare the way,
> Remove every obstruction from
> my people's way.

> *Isaiah 57:14*

At the start of a revolution, five kinds of barriers prevent adoption: ignorance, inertia, complexity, channel, and price.

- **Ignorance.** Reducing ignorance involves making people aware of a new product or service. If the world doesn't know that you've built a better mousetrap, it certainly won't beat a path to your door.

- **Inertia.** This is usually the most challenging and frustrating barrier. It arises after people know there is a better way but still won't adopt it. It can be a crushing experience when

---

* <http://www.acius.com/>

you learn firsthand that most of the world doesn't care if there is a better mousetrap even after they hear about it.

- **Complexity.** The complexity barrier is the difficulty of installing or using a product. If people can't use your product easily, you will fall into the chasm once you get past the hardiest, most dedicated, and most technical customers. No matter how revolutionary your mousetrap, if it takes a whole day or a Ph.D. to set it up, it won't succeed.

EXERCISE

Send one of your products to your parents or your in-laws. See if they can set it up. If not, see if you can explain how to set it up on the telephone.

- **Channel.** If there's no place to buy your product, it will fail. Resistance of the distribution channel to sell and support your product can be deadly. This requires fixing the old channel—but this is usually quite difficult because of its inherent preference for the status quo. It may be easier to create a new channel instead.

- **Price.** "Price"—the scariest word to a revolutionary. On one hand, you should get as much money as possible from early adopters because they derive the most value from it. And you need their money to sustain churning. On the other, if your price eliminates consideration from early adopters, you'll never get to, much less cross, the chasm—a $99 mousetrap won't succeed.

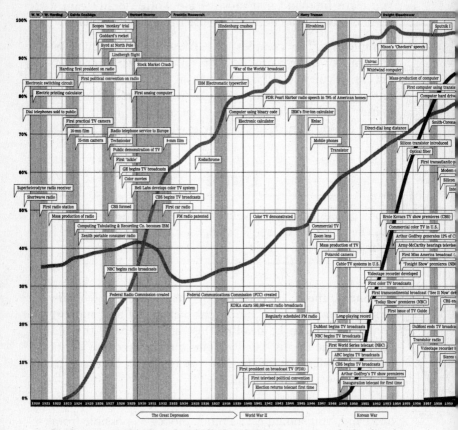

Barriers are coming down faster. Notice the steeper curves of adoption since the 1970's. You can buy a copy of this chart at: <http://info.wsj.com/classroom/catalog/catalog.html>.

Barrier Busting 101

The Big Bang Theory of new product introduction is that you spend a boatload of money on advertising, sales, promotion, and channel incentives. These actions not only break down the barriers, but also establish your product as a category killer. However, the usual real-world sequence of events is this:

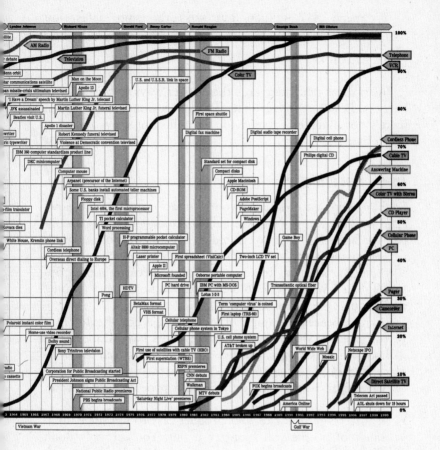

A. Con venture capitalists into giving you $15 million.

B. Hire a big time ad agency.

C. Hire a big time PR agency.

D. Hold a fabulous press conference with $100,000 worth of wine and shrimp.

E. Roll out a print and media campaign.

F. Spend $17 million but miss the ship dates you promised.

G. Go broke.

As it turns out, there are other, better ways to break down barriers. Besides the fact that they cost less and work better, there's not much else to say for the following ways to break down barriers.

Enable test driving

Enabling people to test-drive your product or service is a powerful way to remove or lower barriers to adoption. For example, the WD-40 Company created great awareness of the product by giving away thousands of samples to soldiers in the Vietnam War as a way to keep their weapons clean in the tropical climate.[2] When these soldiers returned home, they wanted the product for civilian uses.

A more peaceful example of test driving is how Revlon provided fingernail-shaped paper samples of its LavenDare line of nail polish. The samples had sticky backs that enabled people to place them on their fingernails to see how they liked the colors.

Creating test-drive samples is good discipline for three reasons:

- It forces you to make your product easy to use since thousands of people will soon try it out. You certainly don't want to have to provide tech support to people who are test driving your product!

- The price to the consumer of a test-drive version is usually very low (if there is a cost at all), so the price barrier is removed. For example, your kid may try the demo version of an expensive piece of software and tell you to buy it. However, she could have never purchased it herself.

- You can sidestep the distribution channel by providing samples directly to people. Hopefully, those people will circle back to the channel and demand that it provide your product.

There are some products where creating a sample is impossible. The test-drive solution for these products is a money-back guarantee. The point is this: Show your prospects that you think they are smart, so you won't try to bludgeon them into becoming a customer. Enable them to test drive, taste, sample, and experience your revolution. Then let them decide for themselves if they want to join it.

Create a sense of ownership

People don't erect barriers to the adoption of a product in which they have a sense of ownership. Ownership, in this instance, is not about equity or title, but a psychological bond with a product someone helped design.

I've done this several times when designing software. Journalists and reviewers gave me feedback about how to change a piece of software, and assuming I could convince the programmer (which was not always the case), I tried to accommodate their suggestions.

Were the reviewers' ideas significant improvements? Not really. Would it take a lot to change the software? Not really. But making this change flattered them and reduced (but did not eliminate, as I came to find out) the likelihood that they would pan a product that they "designed."

Bottom line: Determine who is likely to erect barriers and get them to help you refine your product or service. They may have ideas to significantly improve it. Even if they don't, they are a lot less likely to try to prevent its adoption.

Make Matterhorns out of mountains

This is a page out of the recommendations of a marketing firm in Silicon Valley named Regis McKenna Inc.* It recommends that you make a Matterhorn out of a mountain by positioning a revolutionary product or service "outrageously."

---

*<http://www.mckenna-group.com/>

Outrageous positioning is intended to shock people into recognizing the potential impact of your product or service—thus, it is meant to reduce the ignorance and inertia barriers. However, don't expect people to believe you hook, line, and

PRODUCT OR SERVICE	OUTRAGEOUS POSITIONING
Lexus*	This car is better than a Mercedes[†] or BMW.[‡]
Bose[§] AM/FM Radio	Listening to this radio is better than being at the concert hall.
Silicon Graphics[‖] Workstation	Anyone can make movies as well as George Lucas with this computer.
Southwest Airlines[#]	Cheaper and faster than driving.

sinker. Your goal is to catalyze curiosity: "How can they make this outrageous claim?"

Not every company can use this tactic. There has to be an element of truth to your claim, and your company needs to have a solid reputation. Outrageous positioning is a wink between a credible company and its supportive customers—it is not hucksterism.

Glom on to a bandwagon

Glomming on to a bandwagon means riding a larger force or trend. The bandwagon can help break down ignorance and inertia for everyone—your competition included—because, as the saying

---

*<http://www.lexus.com/>

[†]<http://www.mercedes.com/>

[‡]<http://www.bmw.com/>

[§]<http://www.bose.com/>

[‖]<http://www.sgi.com/>

[#]<http://www.iflyswa.com/>

goes, "a rising tide floats all dopes." Or, even better, create the bandwagon and enable other revolutionaries to jump on yours.

Recently, the mother of all bandwagons has been "the Internet." This tide has floated hundreds of hardware, software, and service boats. And the hardware, software, and service boats added so much value (or took up so much space) that they enabled the tide to rise even more.

The key is to find bandwagons that are irresistible concepts, such as empowering the disenfranchised, democratizing anything, and improving education and literacy.

EXERCISE

Match the revolution to the bandwagon.

Charles Schwab	Empowering information flow
The Internet	Democratizing investments
Cellular phones	Friction-free capitalism
Costco	Freedom and connectivity

Or, Do Things the Old-Fashioned Way

Because I have a bias towards pie-in-the-sky product development, much of this book presumes that if you build a revolutionary product, "they will come." I don't even define who "they" are. However, there are two additional ways to create products and services: Focus on a subset and create a subset.

These two methods merit discussion in this chapter because they avoid, rather than break down, barriers by closely aligning with customer needs from the start.

Focus on a subset of customers

For Fletcher Music Centers in Florida, organs had always been the top-selling item. However, during the 1980s, sales of organs dropped dramatically, and Fletcher found its 1990 profits at an all-time low. The company decided to change its tune and focus on what it had always done best: sell organs.

This decision came despite the fact that organ sales had gone from 250,000 units in the late 1970s to 14,000 by 1990.[3] However, home organ sales had the highest profit margins, and organ buyers tended to upgrade to newer organs as their playing skills increased.

Fletcher discovered that the average age of organ customers was seventy, and they had trouble with the organ's complicated technology and small buttons. Also, they wanted their organs to look like a piece of beautiful furniture, not a plastic high-tech gizmo. The most revealing discovery was that playing the organ gave customers self-worth, companionship with other players, and a real involvement in something.

Seniors did not like the new models of organs coming from Japan, which were laden with technology but not very user-friendly. Fletcher found a company in Italy willing to manufacture the first organ developed for the senior market. Fletcher spent more than a year and $250,000 in development costs to create this organ named the Estey.

In addition to designing a product for this subset of people, Fletcher included free lifetime lessons for people who purchased an organ as well as social activities such as free group lessons. At these lessons, customers meet other people, make friends, and have dinner.

Once in fear of its survival, Fletcher, after the introduction of the Estey and Fletcher's change in focus on a subset of customers, has become the world's largest retailer of home organs. In 1993 the Estey accounted for about 25 percent of all home organs sold in the United States. Creating the Estey and marketing programs for seniors meant that Fletcher had almost no barriers to break down.[4]

Create a subset of customers

Dave & Buster's has opened ten entertainment centers across the country where "big kids" go to play games. This company has created its own niche. The Dave & Buster's facilities are 50,000- to 60,000-square-foot entertainment centers designed for twenty-five- to forty-four-year-olds. No unsupervised minors are allowed, and no one under twenty-one years old is allowed after ten P.M.

These centers are upscale, elegant establishments that go beyond traditional teenager-infested arcades. For example, the billiard room features turn-of-the-century billiard tables of solid mahogany with mother-of-pearl inlay. The restaurants have linen-tablecloths, and the full-length bar is made of brass and hand-carved wood.

In addition to video games, pinball machines, and virtual reality games, fun-seekers can use linked simulators for down-hill skiing, Jet-Skiing, car racing, motorcycle racing, snow-boarding, and, at some centers, airplane flying. A full-swing golf simulator (complete with speed clocks and real clubs) allows players to try twenty of the world's top golf courses.

Aiming these centers at adults has tapped a whole new market segment that had been surprisingly ignored. Like focusing on a subset, when you create a subset like this, there are few barriers to overcome.

Then Erect Barriers

Ironically, after you've broken down or lowered the typical barriers to adoption of your product, you should build a cocoon around your customers so the competition can't attack you. The goal is to get so close to a segment of customers that they live, die, and stick with you. Here are the major types of barriers that you can build.

- **Exclusivity—the best.** The exclusivity barrier means protecting your product or service by making sure it is, and is perceived as, the best. There may be cheaper products; there may be more pervasive products, but yours is the standard by which everything or everyone else is measured. Examples: Harvard University,* Ritz-Carlton† hotels, and Mercedes.‡

- **Mindshare—the most.** The mindshare barrier causes people to select a product or service in a knee-jerk fashion. Unlike the exclusivity barrier, the product or service need not be the best—only the most obvious selection.§ One indication of a mindshare barrier is when a company's name or its product's name becomes a verb.

EXERCISE

Fill in the blanks.

"I have to get ten copies of this document to a client by tomorrow, so I'm going to Kinko's‖ to _____ them and then _____ them out.

- **Price—the cheapest.** The price barrier means that you are a low-cost producer of a product or service and that you are willing to use this advantage as a weapon. This exchange between Bill Gates of Microsoft and CNET# says it all:

Gates: Now, if I try to raise the price of Windows, then that just makes it easier for people to compete with me in operating systems. The question you should be asking yourself is why do we keep the price of Windows so low? That's what you have to ask

---

*<http://www.harvard.edu/>

†<http://www.ritzcarlton.com/>

‡<http://www.mercedes.com/>

§Microsoft Windows, obviously, fits in this category.

‖<http://www.kinkos.com/>

#<http://www.cnet.com/>

yourself. Only when you understand that will you understand Microsoft.

CNET: But on the issue of OS, you have over 80 percent of the market?

Gates: Why do we keep the price so low? Think about it.[5]

Signaling the willingness to fight on price is often enough to scare off competitors (actually lowering prices and profits is often counterproductive for everyone). In the passage above, Bill Gates is telling potential competitors to back off.

- **Customerization—the closest.** Customerization is a concept coined by Don Peppers and Martha Rogers. It means aggressively and enthusiastically customizing products or services for customers. For example, Japan's Paris Miki* is an eyeglass retailer that takes a digital picture of customers and then shows them what various frames and lens sizes would look like on their faces.[6] Once customers' faces are in Paris Miki's eyeglass database, they probably won't shop elsewhere for frames.

- **Knowledge—the expert.** The knowledge barrier occurs when people acknowledge that your organization is likely to be the expert in a field and that the savings from going to another firm is not worth the risk. The Big Five (or Four or Three or Two or One) accounting firms, for example, position themselves as knowledge experts, so businesses usually hesitate to use a non–Big Five firm. And because so many businesses use Big Five firms, other businesses are afraid not to because it makes them look small, stupid, or less legitimate.

- **Infrastructure—the big picture.** One of the reasons Thomas Edison is so famous is that he understood the big picture. While others were perfecting an electrical lamp and tinkering with various types of filaments, he understood that

---

*<http://www.paris-miki.com/>

replacing gas lanterns would take an infrastructure of "efficient electrical generation, wiring, metered distribution, sockets, fuses, and fixtures."[7] Envisioning and controlling the big picture enabled Edison to create a formidable barrier to the competition.

Incidentally, Thomas Edison was not only a big-picture and technical person, he was also a business person. By 1883, a mere four years after beginning experiments on electric lights, the Edison Electric Light Company had 215 patents, and another 307 were pending. He not only obtained these patents, but he vigorously defended them in court—creating another large barrier. By 1885 his company was producing 75 percent of the electric lamps in the United States.[8]

- **Alliances—the buddy.** The Automobile Association of America (AAA*) requires tow trucks to use spacer blocks to lift cars high enough so that the towing chains don't make contact with front fenders. These blocks are simple devices that are made by a company that uses disabled workers. AAA could probably find a cheaper vendor, but the good publicity of using disabled workers and the bad publicity of changing vendors precludes such a search. Thus, this relationship has a terrific built-in barrier.[9]

Ride the Tornado

If you break down the barriers and delight many customers, then your product or service will become the safe, no-brainer buy. You've made it across the chasm. Now demand for your product goes into hypergrowth. Geoffrey Moore calls this period the Tornado, and the business strategy at this time is "to grant supply as quickly and efficiently as you possibly can."[10]

At this point you should drive price points lower and gain as much market share as you can. You're trying to build an

---

* <http://www.aaa.com/>

installed base that's bigger than anyone else's because you can milk an installed base for a decade. This is the good news.

The bad news is that you'll probably become the status quo–perpetuating scumbag that you once despised. (But at least you'll be a rich scumbag.) If you have the foresight, you'll realize that somewhere two guys in a garage are plotting your demise, so you'd better think different and innovate again.

Readings for Revolutionaries

Crossing the Chasm—Marketing and Selling High-Tech Products to Mainstream Customers, Geoffrey A. Moore, HarperBusiness, 1995, ISBN: 0887307175.

Inside the Tornado—Marketing Strategies from Silicon Valley's Cutting Edge, Geoffrey A. Moore, HarperBusiness, 1995, ISBN: 0887307655.

Mastering the Dynamics of Innovation, James M. Utterback, Harvard Business School Press, 1996, ISBN: 0875847404.

5

Make Evangelists, Not Sales

A woman is often measured by the things she cannot control. She is measured by the way her body curves or doesn't curve.

By where she is flat or straight or round. She is measured by 36–24–36 and inches and ages and numbers. By all the outside things that don't ever add up to who she is on the inside.

And so if a woman is to be measured, let her be measured by the things she can control. By who she is and who she is trying to become because as every woman knows, measurements are only statistics, and statistics lie.

Nike* ad

The Macintosh Evangelism Phenomenon

Evangelism comes from the Greek words *eu* ("well" or "good") and *angello* ("to announce" or "to report"). And

---

*<http://www.nike.com>

that's what I did for Apple. My good news was that there was a new personal computer that would make people more creative and productive. People would no longer need either a Ph.D. in computer science, an information services staff, or infinite patience.

Since I was an employee of Apple, you could contend that I was a hired gun and therefore don't count. However, no one can deny that Apple is blessed by the allegiance and support of tens of thousands of "raging, inexorable thunderlizard"* Macintosh evangelists.

These evangelists made Macintosh successful throughout the world. They weren't employees or stockholders, but they believed that Macintosh was good news and told people about it. They formed user groups of customers, conducted free demonstrations, taught Macintosh classes, and straightened up the Macintoshes on display in stores around the world.

You should be so lucky to have evangelists like we did. They can enable you to change the world by carrying the flag for you at times and in places that your company cannot. They will round out and supplement your product where it is weak—for example, providing technical support when you're unable or unwilling to. They will also confound your competition when it tries to woo them away with bribes and inferior products.

EXERCISE

Find 10,500 Americans. Convince them to camp through the winter in Valley Forge with little food or supplies. Don't pay them. General Washington succeeded at this because:

A. He offered his soldiers stock options.

B. He gave out great tchotchkes at the Continental Congress.

---

*This brilliant quote was stolen from Steve Roth.

C. His support staff was all French.

D. At the time, all U.S. programs were incompatible with a monarchy.[1]

Evangelism FAQ (Frequently Asked Questions), Part I

The first 90 percent of a revolution is creating the product or service; the second 90 percent is evangelizing it. At the beginning of a revolution, you need evangelists, not sales, because leverage spreads news. To bring you up to speed on evangelism as quickly as possible, here are the answers to the most common questions about evangelism as a secular, business technique.

Q. What is evangelism?

A. Evangelism is the process of getting people not just to buy but to *believe* in your product, service, or company so much that they are compelled to make converts for you.

Q. What is the starting point of evangelism?

A. The starting point is a great product or service (DICEE) that empowers people and improves their lives. Customers must be able to say, "This is good. This makes the world a better place."

Q. How is evangelism different from word-of-mouth advertising?

A. Every product or service that catalyzes evangelism has good word-of-mouth advertising, but every product or service that has good word-of-mouth advertising doesn't necessarily catalyze evangelism. Word-of-mouth advertising is the precursor of evangelism, but evangelism is more proactive and aggressive.

Q. Can evangelists apply their skills to any product?

A. No, people can evangelize only products that they believe in. Don't hire evangelists from one company and expect them to be as effective with your product unless they have come to love it.

Q. Are evangelists born or made?

A. Evangelists are made (otherwise, how could I sell books?). Anyone can be an evangelist if he creates or is captivated by a life-changing product or service. One is not born "evangelistic."

Q. How is evangelism different from sales?

A. Evangelists have the best interests of the other person at heart. Salespeople have their own best interests at heart. Most evangelists for a product are not employees or stockholders of the company that sells the product.

Q. Are there products that can't be evangelized?

A. A good marketer will tell you that no product is a commodity. A good evangelist will tell you that no product can't be evangelized if it's good news to somebody. Evangelize-ability is in the eye of the beholder.

The Stages of Evangelism

When we began evangelizing Macintosh in 1984, we didn't know what we were doing. Ignorance was bliss because it allowed us to seek and garner support from companies and people that traditional sales and marketing techniques would have ignored. Now, with the benefit of fourteen years of experience, I'm not so ignorant about evangelism and have come up with these stages.

Add emotions to facts

Evangelism starts with a great product or service. The features of a product or a service that make it great are the "facts." These facts are measured in units like megahertz, horsepower, megabytes, BTUs, feet, and inches. Many people think that success is calculated by this classic formula:

$$\text{Success} = \frac{\text{Facts}}{\text{Price}}$$

There are two ways to increase Success: Increase the numerator (Facts) or decrease the denominator (Price). Increasing Facts means adding more features that consumers want, so that your product or service is bigger, faster, or more functional. Decreasing Price means charging less for the same set of facts.[2]

Evangelism provides a third method for increasing the numerator: adding Emotions to Facts:

$$\text{Success} = \frac{(\text{Facts} + \text{Emotions})}{\text{Price}}$$

The Nike ad at the start of this chapter is an example. It is an ad for Nike women's aerobic shoes that illustrates how a company can add emotions to facts. The facts of aerobic shoes are its design, testing, and manufacturing, but Nike has made their aerobic shoes transcend facts until they stand for power, efficacy, and independence.

A (bozo) company that hasn't added emotions to facts would say to women, "We have two pieces of cotton, leather, and rubber. You have $100.00. If you give us the $100.00, we'll give you the cotton, leather, and rubber."

Listen and regurgitate

If people are at all receptive to your revolution, they will tell you how to evangelize them. I first noticed this when evangelizing Macintosh to software developers in 1984. At the start of meetings with developers, we used this three-pronged pitch:

- Macintosh is a technological breakthrough. With what-you-see-is-what-you-get printing, pull-down menus, iconic interface, developers can finally create the kind of software they dreamed of.

- Macintosh will expand the market for personal computers and therefore for your software. Because of its radical ease of use, people who wouldn't have considered buying a computer can finally do so.

- Writing Macintosh software is a way to spread your risk. IBM is publishing MS-DOS application software and competing with you, so the market for your software can get extremely crowded.

If there was any interest in Macintosh development, one of these three pitches appealed to the people in the meeting, and they began to resonate with what we were saying. From that point on, we deemphasized the other two pitches and focused on the one that appealed to the developer.

Lesson: Develop a multi-appeal evangelism pitch, explain it briefly, and then observe what resonates because people will tell you how they want to be evangelized.

Let a thousand flowers bloom

We thought we knew which software would make Macintosh successful: a spreadsheet from Lotus, a word processor from MicroPro, and a database from Ashton-Tate. If you know much about Macintosh software, then you know that we were zero for three on this scorecard.

Meanwhile, an unknown person from an unknown company with an unknown product showed up at Apple for an appointment with the LaserWriter product manager. The unknown person was Paul Brainerd, his company was Aldus Corporation,* and his product was PageMaker. PageMaker spawned a field of flowers called desktop publishing, and desktop publishing saved Apple Computer.

No one at Apple foresaw the market for desktop publishing (despite what you may have read in other books about Apple).

---

* <http://www.adobe.com/>

No one had a vision to remove people's pots of glue, Rapidographs, rulers, and razor blades (AKA analog crap) and replace them with a Macintosh, LaserWriter, and PageMaker (AKA digital crap). No one at Apple wrote a specification for PageMaker, and no one told me to go evangelize such a product.

PageMaker was a gift. It was a flower that bloomed. We weren't looking for it, and we didn't plan it. It shows how the ultimate use of a product can be unrelated to its creator's intentions. For example, did you know that the telephone was first used to broadcast concerts in Budapest? And that Edison pushed the phonograph as a business correspondence tool?

Lesson: Sow many seeds and let a thousand flowers bloom. Let people use and abuse your product in ways that you never envisioned. Do not limit the use of your product to your vision because an unforeseen use may be your PageMaker (NicheMaker?) and save your company.

EXERCISE

James Watt applied the steam engine to:

    A. Powering locomotives.

    B. Pumping water out of mines.

    C. Pumping air to undersea divers.

    D. Driving conveyor belts in factories.

Flow with the go!

If you're fortunate enough to have some flowers grow, the next step is to flow with what goes. That is, to seize the niche by developing a complete solution for it and letting your product achieve its full potential. Consider these unexpected origins of several everyday things:

Atlee Burpee and Company.[*] Washington Atlee Burpee was a chicken expert. While in high school, he authored several articles in poultry journals and operated a poultry mail-order business out of his parents' home. He expanded the business to include raising livestock and later started selling seeds in 1878, so that his customers could raise high-quality food for their animals.

Much to Burpee's surprise, the orders for seeds were greater than the orders for livestock. He focused his catalog on selling seeds for vegetables, fruits, and flowers. (Let a thousand cucumbers bloom?) Burpee's company went on to become a famous provider of seeds while chickens and cows went by the wayside.[3]

SOS Soap Pads. In 1917 Edwin W. Cox was a door-to-door salesman of aluminum pots in San Francisco. Sales were terrible because people had yet to learn of the advantages of aluminum cookware, so Cox needed an introductory gift to entice housewives to allow him to show them his products.

He knew that housewives were having difficulty removing food that had stuck to pans, so he tinkered around with dipping steel wool pads into a soapy solution. After receiving many requests for his free soap-pad gifts from his customers, Cox stopped selling cookware and started selling pads. His wife referred to the pads as "Save Our Saucepans," and SOS pads were born.[4]

Kleenex. During World War I, cotton was in short supply, so Kimberly-Clark[†] invented an absorbent material called Cellucoton for bandages and gas-mask air filters. After the war, the company positioned sheets of the material as a glamour product: a cold-cream tissue to remove makeup used by Hollywood and Broadway stars. It was called "Kleenex Kerchiefs, the Sanitary Cold Cream Remover."

As a cold cream remover, the product did well, but customers started telling the company that they were using the product as a disposable handkerchief. In 1921 a Chicago

---

[*]<http://www.burpee.com/>

[†]<http://www.kimberly-clark.com/>

inventor named Andrew Olsen invented a pop-up tissue box—making Kleenex a more complete product.

By 1930 Kimberly-Clark's management was confused and divided, so it conducted a study in Peoria, Illinois. Customers were enticed to return one of two coupons for a free box of Kleenex. One coupon said, "We pay to prove there is no way like Kleenex to remove cold cream." The other said, "We pay to prove Kleenex is wonderful for handkerchiefs." Sixty-one percent of the coupons that were redeemed were the handkerchief version—and we've been blowing our noses on Kleenex ever since.[5]

These three examples illustrate the concept of flowing with what's going. Each was a case of serendipity leading to new opportunities. Once opportunities become evident, embrace your good fortune and develop a complete product to serve the unforeseen market.

EXERCISE

Write an essay answering this question: Why is it better to be lucky than smart (assuming you're smart enough to know when you're lucky)?

Provide an easy first step

When things start flowing, provide an easy first step for adoption because revolutionary change threatens many people and therefore creates resistance. You need to provide a smooth, easy, and flat adoption curve for your early converts.

For example, before electric light bulbs became the standard light source, gasoline lamps were widely used. In 1900 William Coleman, law student turned salesman, was selling a new brand of gasoline lamps in Kingfisher, Oklahoma. After approximately sixty sales calls, he could not understand why he had sold only two lamps to a town full of after-dark shopkeepers. The local saloon owner told him that another salesman had sold dozens of gasoline lamps that became clogged with carbon and stopped working after the salesman had left town.[6]

Faced with a distrustful group of customers who were not interested in being duped a second time, Coleman revised his approach. He realized he wasn't selling a product, but the benefit of keeping stores open longer, so he rented the lamps to business people. Instead of asking customers to purchase the lamp upfront for $15, he rented them for $1 per week, with a money-back guarantee should the lamp not work.

The service-contract idea succeeded because it was less risky for retailers, and they allowed Coleman to install all twelve of his demonstration lanterns. Today, electric bulbs are the standard light fixture in America, but long before this transition was complete, Coleman* retargeted his marketing to sell gas lamps to campers, fishermen, and other outdoorsy folks.

Ninety-three years after Coleman's efforts, Menlo Park Presbyterian Church of Menlo Park, California, illustrated the concept of an easy first step again. When the church added large video screens and video monitors to its sanctuary so that its 5,000 members could easily see the words of hymns and performers, it introduced this high technology in stages, the first of which was showing the cherubic faces of babies being baptized. Who could argue against this?

Evangelism Frequently Asked Questions, Part II

This is part II of the Evangelism FAQ. It contains the answers to more advanced questions about evangelism.

Q. How can I tell if someone will be a good evangelist for my product or cause?

A. "... Blessed are those who have not seen and yet believe."[7]
The most important quality is that the person loves your product and believes in it. This factor, more than educational background or work experience, will determine the person's suc-

---

*<http://www.coleman-eur.com/>

cess as an evangelist. Thus, pick someone who loves your product over someone who has a great background but no passion for your product.

One additional thought about finding evangelists: The best evangelists for a product will find you—you don't have to find them. They will hunt you down and try their damnedest to get a job at your company.

Q. How can I determine if someone is at all open to my cause?

A. You'll see it in their eyes: They either get it or they don't. They will also get it in the first five minutes or they'll never get it. And if they don't get it right away, no matter how seemingly important they are to the success of your product, move on to greener pastures.

Q. Many companies use the job title "evangelist" these days—how can you tell if these people are truly evangelistic?

A. The acid test is whose best interest they have at heart: their company's or the people they're trying to evangelize. An evangelist has the latter's.

Q. Ownership is important for an evangelistic organization—how do you build a sense of ownership?

A. Call me naïve, but you don't *build* a sense of ownership. Ownership is either there or not as a reflection of reality, so if you want a sense of ownership, make sure people's contributions are used. You can't fake ownership.

Q. How do you sustain interest as an evangelist or as a manager of evangelists?

A. Evangelists are thrill junkies. Once a cause achieves success it is difficult to sustain interest. Three to five years is the limit to bleeding-edge evangelizing, then evangelists have to move on to a different challenge. Recognize this and plan for it.

Q. How does an evangelist avoid looking like a fanatic?

A. This question is a frame, and I refuse to be framed. It pre-supposes that looking like a fanatic is bad, so you want to avoid it. It may not be. The definition of a fanatic is being "unreasonably zealous."

I'm not advocating tying a white bandanna with a rising sun on it around your head and strapping yourself into a plane, but there are times and places to be unreasonably zealous. Status quo–perpetuating people, *nota bene*, may be rightfully accused of being "unreasonably resistant to change."

Q. What is the hardest thing you, as an evangelist, ever had to do?

A. Admit to myself that despite all the evangelism that I did, Microsoft Windows was going to control the world.

Readings for Revolutionaries

Panati's Extraordinary Origins of Everyday Things, Charles Panati, HarperPerennial, 1987, ISBN: 0060964197.

Selling the Dream—How to Promote Your Product, Company, or Ideas and Make a Difference Using Everyday Evangelism, Guy Kawasaki, HarperBusiness, 1992, ISBN: 0887306004.

6

Avoid Death Magnets

The regularity of a habit is generally in proportion to its absurdity.

Marcel Proust

A Lesson from the National Training Center

"Death magnet" is a term coined by Jim Jones, a former M60 tank company commander.[1] He and his tank unit came up with it while at the U.S. Army's National Training Center* at Fort Irwin, California. At this facility, visiting Army brigades engage in "direct fire simulations"† with the home team to increase their battle readiness.

Jones noticed a bizarre thing: Visiting tank commanders drove through areas where they had seen other tanks "killed" during the training exercise. At times, there were so many "dead" vehicles in places that those still moving could barely pass through, and yet they kept going there. He called these areas "death magnets."

Tanks have great difficulty moving quickly through mountainous or wooded terrain, and they can be stopped by rivers,

---

*<http://www.irwin.army.mil/>

†<http://www.irwin.army.mil/command/sld028.htm>

canyons, and canals. Thus, tank commanders are inclined to travel through plains and valleys and along highways and roads. Knowing this, the enemy can use the terrain and its obstacles to funnel the opposing force into kill zones. But as any (living) soldier with battle experience will tell you, "The easy way is mined." The easy way is a death magnet too.

There are death magnets in business—the traditional habits and patterns of thinking that continue to seduce companies. Like successful tank commanders, revolutionaries have to avoid them. Here is an explanation of the ten most common ones.

Death Magnet #10: First, pick the low-hanging fruit

Death-magnet thinking goes like this:

The nerds, geeks, and propeller heads who are early (or premature adopters) will buy almost any new gizmo. They are low-hanging fruit, so take their money and their credibility since the picking is easy.

First of all, this analogy is not even AC (agriculturally correct). If you pick the low-hanging fruit first, then you're climbing up the ladder with a heavy bag. Also, the fruit that's higher up are in the sun more, so they are riper. They should be picked first, not the low-lying ones.[2]

Without jumping through too many hoops, you can find business analogies to these two agricultural findings.

- **Climbing with a heavy bag.** Early adopters are a scary bunch. They love new features, so they will request more bells and whistles in your product, and they become a heavy bag. If you try to explain that you're trying to keep your product simple and relevant for novices, they interpret this as unresponsiveness or stupidity.

- **Other fruit is riper for your product.** If you've created a revolutionary new power tool that makes carpentry easy, professional carpenters who know a lot about power tools may seem like easy sales. But they will also tend to be more conservative about what they buy in the way of new tools—indeed, not wanting to admit they need a revolutionary new tool. The riper fruit may be weekend warriors who haven't yet mastered carpentry and therefore see the value of easy-to-use tools.

As I said in Chapter 4, "Break Down the Barriers," I was president of a software company that published a high-end relational database called 4th Dimension. We initially picked the low-hanging fruit: database professionals and programmers who loved our product's power and breadth of features. From the get-go, these customers pushed us for more features, so we could never focus on ease of use and sell the product to a broader market of less-technical folks.

In general, problems occur when you extrapolate your experience with low-hanging fruit to the rest of the market. You'll find that a product that's good for this obvious audience is too complex for "Main Street," and what's good for "Main Street" is too wimpy for low-hanging fruit. Pick the fruit that's strategic, not necessarily just hanging low.

Death Magnet #9: "Our product sucks less"

Deluding yourself by comparing your product to previous versions or to the competition's offering is the "our product sucks less" death magnet. Previous versions of your product or the competition's may have been pathetic. For example, the Windows versions of many DOS programs are tremendous relative improvements. However, if you take the perspective of a new user, the software is still too hard to use.

Your product may suck less, and thus be relatively better, but is it good enough in absolute terms? Companies in this enraptured state leave opportunities for companies who are more in touch with the realities of the market. Success belongs to the companies that compare the latest version to the entire set of solutions for the problem and to the entire set of customer needs.

As a rule of thumb, revolutionaries should strive to make the optimal solution feasible—as opposed to making the feasible solution optimal.

Death Magnet #9a: Creeping adulteration

The creeping adulteration death magnet is related to "our product sucks less." It means making your product suck a little more in order to save a lot of costs: "Let's make a version that is 95 percent as good but costs 50 percent less to make."

Suppose a brewery decides to change its recipe so that its beer is almost as good but much cheaper to manufacture. With this new product, it can fight on price. But the competition matches the price, so the company decides to make the beer even cheaper while slightly reducing quality—and so on until it ruins the product.

Do this for a few cycles, and you're left with dishwater that isn't saleable, let alone revolutionary. This is what happened to Schlitz in the 1970s.[3]

Death Magnet #8: The budget is king

Has this happened to you? An opportunity presents itself to your company. It involves some risk (AKA added expense), but the upside is tremendous. When you try to acquire additional funds, however, you're turned down with the mantra, "We don't have the budget."

Never mind that this is a good opportunity. Never mind that the marginal revenue will exceed the marginal cost. Never mind that you could shift money over from other, less important areas. The knee-jerk, unthinking reaction is, "No can do." Welcome to the "budget is king" death magnet.

In reality, the budget is seldom the real problem. Budget is king is a symptom of lack of leadership, poor communication, and undue political infighting.

- **Leadership.** I have worked at Apple during some of the heydays of management ineptness. When there was good leadership, budgets were living documents that changed as conditions and opportunities changed. When there wasn't leadership, budgets became the managers of the company. They were practically referred to as people: "Budget said we can't do this."

- **Communication.** When the leadership of a company fails to communicate strategic direction (either because they can't communicate or they have nothing to communicate), budgets reign. Since no one is telling people which projects and markets are important, they assume that the relative amount of money allocated for activities reflects the company's proper priorities.

- **Infighting.** During times of political infighting and factioning within a company, budgets become treaties and the lines of demarcation. They communicate the Mason-Dixon Line between Northern marketing and Southern engineering, and Eastern capital budgets and Western service contracts—subjugating the fact that a company should be one country.

Here are two real-world examples (I have removed the company names to protect the guilty).

First, a delivery company scheduled an airplane crew to fly back on a commercial airline flight that was $50 cheaper per person but lasted two and a half hours longer than another flight. The overtime costs of the two and a half hours far exceeded the $50 saving, but that didn't matter because it came from a separate budget.

Second, a car factory switched from a budget with fixed and variable components to one that was completely fixed to better control costs. However, there were parts of the factory budget that you'd like to see increase—such as energy costs as more cars were produced in response to greater sales. Unfortunately, with a fixed budget, building more cars meant budget overruns. The cure? Sell fewer cars![4]

Budget is not king. Budget is serf, but only if the king, queen, princes, and princesses are working together for the welfare of the land.

Death Magnet #7: We must be conned-sistent

Consistency can be good. It enables people to live without undue distraction, disruption, and disarray. Thus, consistency is associated with intellectual and moral stability and sound judgment. However, the positive offshoots that make consistency appear so valuable discourage independent thought and make consistency a death magnet.

Robert B. Cialdini, a professor of psychology at Arizona State University in Tempe, explains the attractions of blind consistency in his book *Influence: The Psychology of Persuasion.*

The first attraction is that blind consistency offers a shortcut through life. Once you've made up your mind about something, you need not revisit your opinion and analyze new, possibly contradictory, information.[5] Do you remember the management mantra: "No one ever got fired for buying IBM"? It led to suboptimal computer-buying decisions that were ultimately bad for both customers and IBM itself.

The second attraction is peace of mind. Not only can we save time by being blindly consistent, but we also don't have to confront disturbing information.[6] Ignorance is bliss, but it may also be suboptimal. "I don't care if people want to buy things directly from us over the Internet. We've always used resellers."

You don't want to be conned-sistent. You want to be optimal, so when you feel trapped into a decision that you know is wrong, fight it, go the opposite of it, go outside of it, stall for time—do anything except kowtow to it.

EXERCISE

Years ago, a person tried Windows 1.0. It wasn't even close to a Macintosh. For this reason, he never tried a Windows machine again. This person was:

A. Smart.

B. Efficient.

C. Foolishly consistent.

Years ago, a person tried a Macintosh 128K. It was cute but not powerful. For this reason, he never tried a Macintosh again. This person was:

A. Smart.

B. Efficient.

C. Foolishly consistent.

Death Magnet #6: The kiss of yes

If you gave business people the choice of being spread too thin or niched too tightly, most would pick spread too thin. This is the "kiss of yes" death magnet. It means that people are terrified of having their products or services niched—thereby supposedly limiting their growth and upside potential.

Thus they keep saying, "Yes." Yes, Macintosh is a computer for accounting. Yes, Macintosh is a computer for publishing. Yes, Macintosh is a computer for circuit design. Yes, Macintosh is a computer for the accounting departments of *Fortune* 500 companies.

Yes, we will sell computers to schools. Yes, we will sell computers through dealers who sell to schools. Yes, we will sell computers to national accounts. Yes, we will have a national account sales force. Yes, we will sell computers directly through the Internet.

The goal is worthy: getting to "Main Street" where everyone is buying your product because it's already widely accepted. But getting to this state is the problem because you can seldom go directly from revolutionary product to Main Street.

To use Geoffrey Moore's terminology, you have to pay your dues by knocking down barriers and dominating niche markets one at a time. Less is Moore: Saying "No" enables you to focus on niches, totally satisfy them, and then move on to other markets. The shotgun approach of going for every market at once is fraught with danger.

Death Magnet #6a: Our product will be backward compatible

Backward compatibility is the kiss of yes death magnet that plagues high-technology companies. It refers to the desire to make a new hardware run old software or new software run on old hardware. (This isn't restricted to computers. Think of the challenges of making a compact disc player run cassette tapes or cassette players running compact discs.)

The thinking is that you're harming your customers and causing them undue trouble and expense if there isn't backward compatibility. Admittedly, this is in the gray area of Chapter 9, "Don't Ask People to Do Something That You Wouldn't," but it has to be said: Sometimes you need to say "No" to backward compatibility. Here are the reasons:

- It slows down the development process because it is a lot of baggage to carry.

- It suboptimizes the product going forward when compromises are made (and there are enough compromises already).

- It muddies up elegance—just what is this gizmo? The old product with a facelift or a real breakthrough?

The solution to this dilemma is to ensure backward compatibility for *evolutionary* improvements to your product. But when it comes to *revolutionary* leaps, make your product so innovative that people won't care about backward compatibility.

Death Magnet #5: Our brand is a hunting license[7]

Woe is the most frequent result of trying to extend a seemingly all-powerful brand to increase volume. What starts as arrogance ("Our brand is so powerful that we can take it into other markets") usually ends in despair ("We weren't successful in the other markets and tainted our image in our existing ones").

General Motors damaged the Cadillac* brand name by relabeling a Chevrolet† compact car called the Cavalier and selling

---

*<http://www.cadillac.com/>

†<http://www.chevrolet.com/>

it as the Cadillac Cimarron.[8] Gerber looked stupid in the 1970s when it created a line of gourmet food for grown-ups sold in baby food jars called Singles.[9] And Bic, the company that made a name for itself in disposables (pens, lighters, and razors), got flicked when it introduced a perfume called Parfum Bic in the 1980s.[10]

EXERCISE

True or False:

A. Fruit of the Loom* introduced a laundry detergent in 1977.

B. Exxon† entered the office automation business in 1985.

C. Banana Republic launched a travel magazine called *Trips* in 1988.[11]

Death Magnet #4: Outsourcing saves money

In 1995 the management of a large printing company decided to stop writing its own software to manage printing. Instead, it would use off-the-shelf software and integrate these products into the company's workflow using outside contractors.[12]

After the decision, the company began to lose its programmers. These people had been with the company for years and understood the printing business. Contractors who knew little about the company and its customers replaced them. When the programmers were employees, it was easy to communicate with the person in the next cubicle. Now its projects became late, over budget, and error-prone—all because management fell for the death magnet of reducing overhead by outsourcing.

Outsourcing can work in situations where the need is tem-

---

*<http://www.fruit.com/>

†<http://www.exxon.com/>

porary (for example, setting up a once-a-year sales meeting) or functions that are not and cannot become part of your competitive advantage. For example, high-technology firms like Oracle* outsource the operation of their photocopying centers to a firm like Xerox Business Systems.† No matter how great Oracle became at managing photocopying centers, this skill wouldn't be a competitive advantage.

However, in general, outsourcing is a short-sighted method to fool yourself into thinking you're saving money while you're spending more money and possibly trashing your core competencies.

Death Magnet #4a: We have to work all the time

Working all the time is not an intended consequence of vetting the outsourcing death magnet because excessive hours is a death magnet too:

- You need to save some mental, physical, and emotional resources for enhancing your product after you ship. A revolution is a triathlon, not a hundred-yard dash—it requires long-distance stamina and multiple skills such as creating, churning, and evangelizing.

- If you're working all the time, you have fewer opportunities to gather, digest, and spread information, to "eat like a bird and poop like an elephant." (This will make sense when you read the next chapter.)

- Measuring the amount of time spent on the job is usually easier than measuring the results you're achieving. It's very easy to succumb to peer pressure to be at the office earlier and leave later than others. It's also easy to convince yourself that you're a hero since you're working so long and hard.

---

*<http://www.oracle.com/>

†<http://www.xerox.com/>

Try this think-different approach: Mandate that your building will be open for set hours such as eight A.M. to six P.M. Let no one work in the building before or after these hours. When the supply of office time is finite (that is, ten hours), you are likely to find that people focus on their work, meetings are shorter, and everyone is healthier.

Death Magnet #3: Monkey see what gorilla do

While I was searching for examples for this book, a member of the Rules for Revolutionaries Internet mailing list named Lewis Moore told me about his experience as the administrative assistant to the resident director of the Cyprus Island division of Cyprus Mines Corporation.* This is the inside story of the demise of this company.

In 1917 a mining engineer was sent to the Middle East to find the legendary gold mines of King Solomon. After looking all over the Sinai and Egypt, he ended up on the island of Cyprus. The locals took pity on him because he was running out of money and showed him a few outcrops of color on a hill. The engineer recognized that copper lurked just beneath the surface. He had discovered a veritable mountain of copper only ten miles from a good harbor.

Cyprus Mines Corporation was the outcome. It thrived from the end of World War I until the mid-sixties, when, fat with idle cash, the company hired a new president without a mining background. Among his first acts, he expanded and redecorated the corporate offices. Emulating big conglomerates, he began a diversification plan by investing in timber production in the Northwest, a cement plant in Hawaii, a shipping company, and big iron-ore projects in Australia and Canada.

The end result (partly because of a drop in the price of copper) was that the company plunged heavily into debt. Most of the ancillary companies were sold off, most of the people were

---

*<http://www.cyprusamax.com>

let go, and the shell was sold to Amoco.* Amoco let the rest of the company die a slow and painful death.

This happened because a successful monkey wanted to become a gorilla by acting like a gorilla. This is a mistaken notion. Gorillas became gorillas because they *grew* into gorilla-dom. They didn't become gorillas by copying what other gorillas did.

EXERCISE

Suppose your organization is a new software company—a monkey. You want it to be huge—a gorilla—like the mother of all software gorillas, Microsoft. In which area should you copy the gorilla's practices?

    A. Run an impressive image advertising campaign.

    B. Rent 100,000-square-foot booths at trade shows.

    C. Sell only through well-established resellers.

    D. Throw fabulous cocktail party press conferences.

    E. Churn products relentlessly.

Death Magnet #2: Larger market share causes higher profitability, therefore lower your prices

This is the most dangerous and yet commonly accepted death magnet of them all. It's usually espoused by a testosterone-overdosed yuppie who believes that by lowering prices, the company will gain market share, drive out competitors, and achieve greater profitability when it controls the market.

There are at least three things wrong with this thinking:

- There is a correlation between market share and profitabil-ity, but market share doesn't necessarily *cause* profit-

---

*<http://www.amoco.com/>

ability.* Good products, good marketing, and good service causes profitability *and* high market share too.

- In fact, the factors preventing greater profitability (and market share) may have nothing to do with prices. For example, in 1997, McDonald's† waged a price war‡ with Burger King§ to gain market share (and presumably future higher profitability). However, many people believed it was the quality of its food, not the prices, that was hindering sales. Lesson: Fix what's broken, not what's seemingly easy or obvious.

- Counterintuitive and rule breaking as this may seem, when a market is growing, successful companies may want to lose market share. This is because during a bust (and there's always a bust), these companies may be better prepared to compete because they have not overexpanded and added to overhead costs.[13]

Think of market share as a result, not as a cause. If you have a great product and great customer service, then, as a result, you'll also have a larger market share and healthy profits.

Death Magnet #1: The best product wins

Unto every one that hath shall be given.[14]

If only this were true, Bill Gates would be working at a

---

*For that matter, many executives of profitable companies drive expensive German cars; this doesn't mean that buying all the executives in your company a German car will make it profitable.

†<http://www.mcdonalds.com/>

‡The best book ever written about pricing is *The Strategy and Tactics of Pricing—A Guide to Profitable Decision Making* by Thomas T. Nagle and Reed K. Holden. One great thing about this book is that it sells for $28.50 in hardback and $55 in paperback, and Amazon.com offers no discount for it. I love authors who practice what they preach! (Yes, the paperback costs more than the hardback!)

§<http://www.burgerking.com/>

Starbucks* making espressos and living in a rented apartment. Unfortunately, the best products don't necessarily win if another product is, at a minimum, sufficient plus quick to market, well promoted, and revised (churned) quickly.

Why? Because of the Law of Increasing Returns: The more a product sells, the easier it is to sell. Other products may be better, but people get locked into a product and sales snowball even though it may be inferior.

The classic example is the QWERTY keyboard, which is not the best design for typing efficiency—indeed it was designed to slow down touch typists who were able to type ahead of the old mechanical typewriters! But it came out before other designs, achieved market dominance, and subsequently made the transition from mechanical typewriters to electric typewriters to computers.

Today, no matter how great a new keyboard layout is, it's impossible to establish a new, widespread standard. However—and here is the opportunity for revolutionaries—if a discontinuity such as voice input occurs, then the QWERTY keyboard may go the way of MS-DOS.

EXERCISE

Explain why you agree or disagree with this statement:

"The most common reason people use Windows is that they know it's better than a Macintosh."

Extra credit: Which is the biggest oxymoron?

    A. Apple marketing.

    B. Microsoft innovation.

    C. Family vacation.

---

*<http://www.occ.com/starbucks/>

Death Magnet #1a: A revolutionary product is a substitute for the previous product

The fact that the best product doesn't always win is depressing, but you often have little control over the outcome. On the other hand, if your own shortsightedness cripples your success, then you've really blown it.

The substitution death magnet can cause a blown opportunity. This occurs when you think that your product is merely a substitute for an existing product. For example, the schmexperts in Chapter 2 who convinced IBM to turn down Haloid's photocopy machine probably thought of this gizmo as a substitute for carbon paper or mimeograph machines.*

In fact, photocopiers opened up and created new markets that were inconceivable for carbon paper and mimeograph machines. After all, limit-busting, market-creating, radical change is what revolutions are all about.

Why Does Folly March On?

In her book *The March of Folly*, historian and Pulitzer prize–winning author Barbara Tuchman explained why death magnets continue to march on. (Her term for death magnets is "folly," which she defines as "the pursuit of policy contrary to the self-interest of the constituency or state involved.")

For a policy to be considered folly, Tuchman stipulates that it must meet three criteria:

- ". . . it must have been perceived as counter-productive in its own time, not merely by hindsight."

- ". . . a feasible alternative course of action must have been available."

---

*Authors should thank their lucky stars because photocopiers made multiple submissions of manuscripts possible. And multiple submissions of manuscripts led to bidding wars and higher advances.

- ". . . the policy in question should be that of a group, not an individual ruler, and should persist beyond any one political lifetime."[15]

Does this description sound familiar? It's a pity that Tuchman didn't lower herself to write about business because we would have benefited immensely. Luckily, she explained the two reasons why "wooden-headedness," to use Tuchman's term, continues to march on:

- ". . . assessing a situation in terms of preconceived fixed notions while ignoring or rejecting any contrary signs."

- ". . . the refusal to benefit from experience . . . "[16]

When business leaders learn these two lessons, they and their companies will start defying death magnets. Until then, there will always be opportunities for revolutionaries to succeed as long as they don't fall for death magnets themselves.

Readings for Revolutionaries

Influence: The Psychology of Persuasion, Robert B. Cialdini, William Morrow, 1993, ISBN: 0688128165.

Managing Brand Equity—Capitalizing on the Value of a Brand Name, David A. Aaker, The Free Press, 1991, ISBN: 0029001013.

The March of Folly: From Troy to Vietnam, Barbara W. Tuchman, Ballantine Books, 1992, ISBN: 0345308239.

The Strategy and Tactics of Pricing—A Guide to Profitable Decision Making, Thomas T. Nagle and Reed K. Holden, Prentice Hall, 1994, ISBN: 0136690602.

PART 3

CREATE LIKE A GOD.

COMMAND LIKE A KING.

WORK LIKE A SLAVE.

7

Eat Like a Bird, Poop Like an Elephant

. . . Find out what today's consumer wants and today's retailer is showcasing in small gift shops, toy stores, bookstores, bath and bed areas of department stores. Compare what you find in specialty stores to the mass channels: grocery, discount, Kmart, Von's, Wal-Mart, etc. Talk to people about what they are not finding in stores. What products would they like to see developed in what format and at what cost.

From the job application for product designer positions at Hallmark Cards

Birds Eating? Elephants Pooping?

If someone tells you that you eat like a bird, the implication is that you don't eat much. Yet for their body weight, birds eat a lot. The peripatetic hummingbird, for example, eats the equivalent of 50 percent of its weight every day. (If you're a 200-pound male, imagine eating 100 pounds of food every day!)

Chances are that no one will tell you that you poop like an elephant because elephants poop 165 pounds per day. So far you're probably thinking, "Guy is into the weirdest things. No wonder Apple had so many problems." However, there are two serious messages for revolutionaries in these biological facts.

First, a successful revolutionary relentlessly searches for, consumes, and absorbs knowledge about the industry, customers, and competition. You do this by pressing the flesh of your customers, attending seminars and trade shows, reading journals, and browsing the Internet.

Second, you need to spread the large amount of information knowledge that you've gained—pooping like an elephant. This means sharing information and discoveries with your fellow employees and occasionally even with your competitors.

Principles of Eating

San Francisco cardiologists Meyer Friedman and Ray Rosenman were the first to link competitive, overachieving, impatient, and hostile behavior with cardiovascular disease. These characteristics, now categorized as Type A behavior, are highly correlated with cardiac risk.

During the mid-fifties, Friedman and Rosenman's waiting room furniture exhibited an unusual problem: the fronts of the seat cushions and armrests were constantly in tatters. This prompted their upholsterer to ask, "What the hell is wrong with your patients? People don't wear out chairs this way."

In a perfect avarian world, Friedman or Rosenman would have stopped and analyzed this curious finding. Patients in the waiting rooms of other types of doctors weren't shredding the arms of chairs. There had to be an explanation.

Alas, Friedman confessed that he didn't pay any attention to what the upholsterer said. It was not until five or so years later when formal research showed the link between personality and cardiovascular risk that he remembered the upholsterer's observations.[1] If Friedman had been eating like a bird, he might have seen the link between people who tore up upholstery and the presence of heart disease years earlier.

This example illustrates the first principle of eating (one that

Roy Plunkett's discovery of Teflon in Chapter 1 also illustrated):

Always search for the cause of something unexpected.

Leave the important stuff to amateurs

The Japanese have a saying that the more important a function, the more you should use amateurs. This is the second principle of eating. Nothing is more important than gathering information about your customers and your competition, so you should never leave it to marketing research professionals.

Because of their preference for analysis over synthesis, jargon to common sense, and sophistication over simplicity,[2] marketing research professionals and their stock-in-trade tools create five kinds of problems.

- **Inability to detect and communicate subtle findings.** Suppose that you're the owner of a car dealership (but an amateur researcher), and you watch people in your showroom. You notice two things: First, many people shop with kids, and when the kids get bored, the car buying expedition ends. Second, the first thing that the wives do is look for the cupholders in the car. These are very subtle findings that most market researchers (asking car shoppers to fill out a questionnaire as they leave) would miss—especially the ones with antsy kids who are the people you need to study the most!

- **The loss of unforeseen opportunities.** Continuing with our car dealership example, an amateur would see two opportunities: Build a play area for kids to use while their parents are shopping and draw attention to every cupholder in the car by putting empty Big Gulp soda cups in them. Both these opportunities would be lost in the process of professional market research.

- **Staleness of information.** I would bet that the time lapse between Sam Walton noticing a good practice in a competitor like Price Club* and implementing it in Wal-Mart† was days, if not hours. Professionals however, have to create a report with beautiful charts and long appendices so that everything "looks professional." This is, of course, after the time it takes to negotiate the research project, hire and train people, and collect data.

- **Issues falling through cracks.** The old saying, now updated, is still true: "To a programmer, every problem looks like software." This means that researchers see problems through the perspective of their own specific backgrounds, and problems not addressed by a particular background fall through the cracks.

EXERCISE

Have you ever seen a consultant's report that recommended solutions that were outside his area of expertise?

- **Incomplete distribution of information.** When a company conducts professional research, only a small fraction of the employees read the results—executives, product managers, and marketing folks. Customer service people, research and development engineers, and others downstream might never see it. For sure, the receptionist never sees it. But your receptionist probably shapes customer opinion of your company more than any other employee.

Honda has real-world market research all figured out. It uses the *sangen* or "three actuals" approach: actual product, actual person, actual situation.[3] Here are some real-world examples from other companies:

- **Actual product.** After it opened, Walt Disney spent every weekend at Disneyland. He would slip into shows and rides

---

* <http://www.pricecostco.com/>

† <http://www.wal-mart.com/>

unseen, then offer his critique. He was experiencing the same product as customers.

- **Actual person**. During the Korean War, Kelly Johnson, the leader of the Skunk Works group at Lockheed, took a tour of the Korean battlefront. He traveled over 23,000 miles and visited fifteen air bases to learn firsthand what improvements pilots wanted in their planes.[4]

- **Actual situation**. Alfred Sloan used to take off from General Motors headquarters once per quarter and spend a week selling cars, working in a parts operation, or doing something at a dealership.[5]

Kelly Johnson, the legendary leader of Skunk Works.

Institutionalize pressing flesh

Employees from DuPont's spinning mills visit their customers at the factories where nylon is transformed into bathing suits and brassieres. These DuPont representatives ask the factory operators about quality problems that they might experience when using DuPont's nylon.

This effort was designed to improve the nylon products and to bring more DuPont employees, not just those in management, closer to the customer. Employees at all levels work with customers to "ensure we are doing whatever we can to make them successful," says communications manager Bill Brown. These employees are not given a checklist or set of questions, rather they are "well enough versed in what they do that they know automatically what to ask," according to Brown.

Not only should you use amateurs for gathering information, but, as this DuPont example illustrates, you should institutionalize the process so that it happens regularly. Your organization will benefit in four ways as a result:

- **Employees get better at the process.** They learn who to ask the tough questions and how to know when they get the answer. They also learn how to communicate this information back to the home office and obtain the best results.

- **The information is more reliable.** Since you're not depending on just a few sources—much less sanitized and delayed (but beautifully presented!) professional versions—you can depend on the feedback.

- **Faster solutions to problems.** You'll obtain not only information about problems, but quick solutions to those problems. Employees watching how a customer uses a product can "precipitate" answers because they are aware of the company's capabilities.

- **Customer faith.** The regularity of the process shows both the customer and your employees that "know thy customer" (or competition) isn't this week's management fad.

Institutionalizing the flesh-pressing process provides better and better information. (Consider the difference between what you tell close friends and mere acquaintances.) In fact, in the best cases, you not only get good information, you can also try out new ideas.

EXERCISE

When a new feature movie comes out, the owner of Edwards Theater in Newport Beach, California, stands in the lobby and asks customers what they thought not only about the movie, but also about the facilities and food.[6]

When was the last time you ever met the owner of a movie theater?

Don't ask, just watch

When Philips Consumer Electronics* was developing a portable radio-cassette player for teenagers, called MovingSound, the company conducted focus groups with its potential young customers. The player was designed in two colors, a bright yellow color meant to attract the youth market and classic black.

During the focus groups, the overwhelming majority of the teenagers said they would prefer the yellow color. After the discussion was over, Philips thanked the participants by giving them a free MovingSound player. A pile of yellow players and a pile of black players were placed outside the testing room. Most of the teenagers chose a black player.[7]

This is a prime example of the principle, "Don't ask, just watch." When you ask people what they want, they think about how they should answer; they want to look smart; and they are influenced by what other people say. On the other

---

*<http://www.philips.com/>

hand, when you don't ask them, but simply watch what they do, their actions speak more truly than words.

Even when you're just watching, beware of three effects that can reduce the real-world applicability of your findings:

- If people have allowed you to watch them (because they volunteered or were paid to participate in a study), they are no longer a truly representative sample. For example, 40 percent of the people asked to participate in the "people meter" studies of Nielsen, the television monitoring company, turn the request down.[8] The 60 percent who agree are hardly a random sample.

- If people know that you're watching them, their behavior may change. This is called the Hawthorne effect after a study of workers in a Hawthorne, Illinois, factory in the 1920s. Researchers believed that the mere act of watching workers made them increase output.

- A group of people deciding what they like is not the same as the real-world shopping experience. One person or a small group of people who liked yellow may have dominated the Philips focus group. However, left to their own choice after the group session, the majority of subjects were free to pick the color and most picked black.

Perch in different trees

> Though import [car] sales could hit 425,000 [cars] in 1959, they may never go that high again.*
>
> Business Week, *January 17, 1958*[9]

If you grew up in Lansing, Michigan, in the seventies, you

---

*In 1997, Toyota sold about 397,000 Camrys in the United States. Lesson: never use the word "never." :-)

would have gotten the impression that the whole world owned Oldsmobiles. When you drove on I–96 you would have seldom seen any Japanese cars, so you probably wouldn't have viewed Toyota,* Nissan,† or Honda‡ as a threat to American cars.[10] Staying only in Lansing is perching in only one tree—you may know what's going on in the tree but not in the forest.

If you want to know what is happening in the rest of the forest (and be in business for a long time), perch in different trees from time to time. Force yourself to travel to places you've never been before, shop in stores you never frequented before, eat in restaurants that you've never patronized, read books and magazines that are outside your specific industry, and attend trade shows of other industries.

How can this help? Here's an example. When Lockheed's Skunk Works§ design team encountered broken rubber seals inside engine valves and leaking seals around the cockpit of the U–2 spy plane, they replaced them, but the seals quickly oxidized again in a just few weeks.

The design team couldn't figure out why this was happening until a Skunk Works employee found the answer in the *Los Angeles Times*.‖ The newspaper reported that European-made automobile tires were oxidizing quickly in Los Angeles due to smog in the area. The problem was traced to ozone—a primary component of smog. Because U–2 planes were flying in the part of the atmosphere heavily laden with ozone, the same thing was happening to their seals.[11]

---

*<http://www.toyota.com/>

†<http://www.nissan.co.jp/>

‡<http://www.honda.com/>

§<http://www.lmsw.external.lmco.com/lmsw/html/index.html>

‖<http://www.lats.com/>

EXERCISE

Go to a bookstore (an analog bookstore, not Amazon.com) and browse unfamiliar sections. (If you're like most business people, this would include sociology, philosophy, physics, and biology.)*

Take small bites

I have no elaborate filing system; no database, for instance, and no millions of articles in folders with tags recording their location. I used to maintain such a system and found that I never used it. I hardly ever went back to the files. Instead, I concentrate on educating myself; on passing information through my mind so it affects my outlook: on tuning my attention as if it were an instrument. Sometimes, admittedly, I let articles and reports pile up in stacks; then I sift through the stacks to find what I need. And sometimes I must go back and re-create all the research I did several years before. But that, in itself, is valuable, because in the fields I care about, the facts have changed since I last went to look for them. Don't worry about your files; worry about your perceptions.

Peter Schwartz, The Art of the Long View

Hummingbirds eat as they go; they don't hoard food to eat later. You should act the same way by reading and analyzing information as you get it—before it piles up.[12]

I've found that if I don't read a new book or magazine or explore a Web site that someone referred me to in the first forty-eight hours, then I never do it. Something else always comes up or an even better (supposedly) source of information rears its pretty head.

However, if you read and analyze information as it comes

---

*The ability to browse shelves is why Web-based bookstores will never put traditional (analog) bookstores out of business.

in, your eating habits will improve. You might say that you develop better "taste" as stored information helps you shape and optimize future searches and analyses. As Peter Schwartz says, perceptions are the key.

Become a research librarian . . . or suck up to one

Access to information used to be restricted by either caveat or cost. For example, Dialog Information Services provided access to electronic databases of information. Corporate research librarians were its primary customer because of two barriers: high cost (access to some databases used to cost $300 per hour) and a user interface that only a mainframe programmer's mother could defend.

By 1997 the Internet broke down both these barriers, so birds of all sizes, affiliations, and net worths could eat freely. Essentially, anyone can become a research librarian. Here are six inexpensive ways to do this:

- **Dialog Select.** Dialog Select* was formerly known as Dialog Information Services, but more than its name has changed. It is much easier to use because it is accessible on the Internet via a graphical user interface, and the cost is lower because you can pay on a per view basis. This is the granddaddy of on-line information, with thousands of sources containing very valuable information such as trademark and patent listings.

- **Electric Library.** Electric Library[†] enables you to search through hundreds of newspapers and magazines plus newswires, radio and television transcripts, and major works of literature. Searching through this breadth of publications used to be very expensive and very time consuming.

---

*<http://dialogselect.krinfo.com/>

[†]<http://www.elibrary.com/>

EXERCISE

Can you remember using the *Reader's Unabridged Guide to Periodical Literature*?

- **Ask Jeeves.** Ask Jeeves* allows you to conduct free research too. You enter a question in plain English, then the site enables you to select from a list of matched questions. After you select the closest question, Ask Jeeves takes you to a Web site that provides the best answer.

- **Inquisit.** Inquisit† receives data feeds from over 600 sources such as magazines, newspapers, and press releases. For about $13 per month, you can create software agents that search these data feeds for the kind of information that you specify; then Inquisit sends you e-mail with either a summary or the full-text of the article that contained the information.

- **Internet mailing lists.** An Internet mailing list is a group of people who receive e-mails about a specific subject. These mailing lists are useful for soliciting feedback and trolling for information from people who share a common interest. For example, while writing this book, I operated a Rules for Revolutionaries Internet mailing list that had 600–700 members. I would ask these members for examples to illustrate my concepts and invariably get excellent information. All you need to operate your own Internet mailing list is an Internet connection and software such as LetterRip.‡

- **Usenet discussion lists.** Whereas a specific group of people "subscribe" to Internet mailing lists, there are also ongoing discussions on thousands of topics on Usenet. Anyone can drop into these discussions, post a question, and then wait

---

* <http://www.askjeeves.com/>

† <http://www.inquisit.com/>

‡ <http://www.fogcity.com/>

for answers. One need not formally subscribe to them unlike Internet mailing lists. If you can think of a topic, there's a Usenet discussion list for it. Go to a search engine like Yahoo* and enter a search like "Usenet and country music." You won't believe the quantity of information and expertise that you'll find.

While writing this book, I had this e-mail exchange with someone at an Internet information service called Findout. (The funny reference to Answers.com is because Findout competes with Answers.com.) It illustrates the advantage of using human librarians to do a search. No text-based search engine that I know of would have made the connection to Captain Miller's Medal of Honor that the person from Findout made.

I'm writing a book called Rules for Revolutionaries. *The name of the medal will be an example in the book. Sources Checked: Various French Foreign Legion sites and Answers.com. How's that for a challenge? Show up Answers.com!*

Question #1:

Someone told me that there's a medal given to members of the military for directly disobeying the order of a superior when the superior was wrong. It might be the French Foreign Legion. What country gives this medal and what is the name of the medal?

Answer #1: Hi! Those chumps at Answers.com can't compete with our direct-disobey finding skills . . . Although we didn't locate any reference to this policy being official in any world military organization in our fifteen minutes of research, we may be able to supply you with an alternate explanation.

It seems that, on the auspicious date of July 3, 1863, a certain Captain William Miller disobeyed the order of his

---

* <http://www.yahoo.com/>

brigade commander. This commander ordered his regiment to remain, but Captain Miller ordered a charge, in direct violation of his superior's command. Apparently Miller's was the right decision, because he was awarded a Congressional Medal of Honor. This information was provided courtesy of Ms. Louis Friend at the Institute for Military History.

You can read the full citation for Miller's award at the U.S. Army Center of Military History; just scroll down to the honorable rebel's name. <http://www.army.mil/cmh-pg/mohciv2.htm>

If you have any further questions, please feel free to "Ask Us More," using the button below. Hope this information helps, and thanks for using FINDOUT!

If you can't get to a computer or you're disinclined to become your own research librarian, then do things the old fashioned way: Find and befriend one. Research librarians are working in large companies as well as public libraries. You will be astounded by what these people can find out for you because of their knowledge of and access to books, magazines, journals, and electronic databases.

Tap human carriers

The human brain has a capacity for flexibly restructuring information in a manner that has never been approached by even the most sophisticated computer programs. For truly effective transfer of technical information, we must make use of this human ability to recode and restructure information so that it fits into new contexts and situations. Consequently, the best way to transfer technical information is to move a human carrier.[13]

Professor Thomas J. Allen, MIT Sloan School of Management*

---

*<http://web.mit.edu/afs/athena.mit.edu/org/s/sloan/www/>

Allen documented that one of the best ways to gather information is to hire people from other companies or academia who have knowledge in areas that are important to you.

This concept has two important ramifications: First, beware the sacred cow called "we must reduce turnover" because it may be a death magnet. As long as the amount of turnover is not disruptive, the influx of new employees and loss of old employees may be a positive development for the inflow of new ideas and methods.

Second, the value of new employees is not simply their ability to do the job, but also includes the totality of their knowledge and experience they may bring to the job. Hiring a programmer from Microsoft, for example, yields valuable expertise about churning, testing, and documentation—not just programming.*

Two additional types of human carriers are especially helpful: vendors and government/academic institutions. Vendors are helpful because they are aware of the efforts of companies in similar fields—but *nota bene*: a vendor who will tell you about a customer's efforts will tell other customers about your efforts. Many people who work for government/academic institutions often don't see themselves as competing with private-sector companies. As a result, they are more willing to share knowledge.[14]

Finally, Professor Allen also explains the concept of "gatekeepers."[15] These folks function on two levels: They are internal opinion leaders and external, highly visible "industry leaders." They are typically mid-level managers who exert considerable influence because they are at the nexus of information flow.

Thus, a gatekeeper is a kind of super-carrier who provides considerable influence and information despite the lack of a highfalutin title. It's important to recognize the way they help information flow among employees and how this contributes to your company's success.

---

*And by hiring an executive, you'll gain an expert in antitrust law and the Department of Justice.

Pooping the Apple Way

Apple has an unfortunate history of pooping like a bird, rather than an elephant. For example, if we had aggressively licensed the Macintosh operating system to other companies in 1987, the Macintosh operating system might have become the dominant system in personal computers today. Why were we so seemingly stupid?

The answer is not as clear as hindsight might lead you to believe. We were making $1,000 on every Macintosh. The stock market had a ninety-day perspective on income. It may seem obvious today, but it would have taken great courage and insight to foster erosion of such wonderful margins. How could we tell the investment community that we wouldn't be making much money for the next two years as we "set a standard"? (Of course, one could make the case that making difficult strategic decisions like that is why our execs got the big bucks.)

At the time, IBM had taken the exact opposite approach and created an open standard for the IBM PC. Every company was making money selling IBM PC clones except IBM. Surely, we thought we wanted to avoid a similar outcome.

Finally, *mea culpa*, we were arrogant and French* (that is, led by Jean-Louis Gassée†). We believed we had the best operating system and an insurmountable lead over the competition, so why shouldn't we get the most money for it? We were the creators of the *fine du fine*, the *haute* computer.

EXERCISE

Ask your CFO if Wall Street will understand when profits decline for two years while your company establishes your product as a standard.

---

*Is this redundant?

†<http://www.be.com/>

May the right decision be more obvious to you than it was to us. But if you ever have to make a crucial choice like we did, then use this algorithm:

The more inevitable your type of product or service is, the more you should strive to establish a standard, make less money per unit, and make the big money on volume.

Rightly or wrongly, Apple is usually credited with "inventing" personal computers and the graphical user interface. However, personal computers and the graphical user interface were going to happen even if Apple didn't do it. Thus, we should have pooped like an elephant and licensed the Macintosh operating system to others.

The Joy of Pooping

Luckily, most of the information sharing and spreading decisions you'll have to make will be less risky than Apple's. But for a revolutionary, the attitude should always be, "I poop, therefore, I am" because the more information you give away, the more you get as people come to trust you and see mutual benefits.

A researcher for a medical lab explained the differences between working for a company that maintains an open environment and working for a closed one. I call his little essay "The Joy of Pooping."

> I have worked for two opposing labs. One pooped like a bird, and no one ever shared anything back with us. It was like blazing a trail parallel to the highway. I could see a better way, but nobody would let me on the highway because I had nothing to give back.
>
> I work with an elephant pooper now. And I tell you, I remember everyone who sends us methods, probes, antibodies, etc., and we do everything to reciprocate the favors. It is much more efficient this way.[16]

The computer business provides two recent examples of opening up and spreading information. First, id SOFTWARE

Inc.,* the publisher of the computer game Doom, has enabled people to create weapons, enemies, sounds, and battle scenes as add-ons. This not only enriched the game, but also encourages the creators of add-ons to tell others to buy it. If you search the Internet for Web sites dedicated to Doom, you'll find dozens of supporters.

Second, on January 22, 1998 Netscape Communications Corporation† announced that it would make its browser free and publicly post the source code (that is, the actual lines of programming) for a future version called Netscape Communicator 5.0. Making source code available would enable programmers around the world to change and enhance the Netscape product.

The company took this aggressive action to slow down the adoption of a competitive browser called Internet Explorer from Microsoft. Here's the theory:

- Microsoft is already giving away its browser, so Netscape can't compete with a browser that people have to buy. It might as well give its browser away too.

- Thousands of programmers will take Netscape's source code and create enhanced versions of the Netscape browser as well as new versions.

- No matter how many Microsoft programmers are enhancing Internet Explorer, they are less than the number of programmers on the Internet who will start hacking away at Netscape's product.

- The versions created by the public will be better products for groups of people and companies than the single version of Microsoft's Internet Explorer, and Netscape's browser will survive.

---

*<http://www.idsoftware.com/>

†<http://www.netscape.com/>

This action is a fascinating development in the browser wars. In the first month, there were 250,000 downloads of the source code. Somebody is going to do something cool with it, but if nothing else, Netscape deserves credit for thinking different and making the source code public.

The Principles of Pooping

Here are the four things you need to do to spread (and receive) information in the most efficient ways:

- **Get over the paranoia.** First things first: Stop worrying about the negative effects of spreading information to other parts of your company as well as colleagues and competitors. Sure, be judicious about what you share, but err on the side of sharing too much.

- **Make it simple, correct, and frequent.** Spread efficiently by making the information that you're sharing simple and correct; and do the spreading often. The better and more frequent the information that you provide, the better and more frequent the information you'll get back.[17]

- **Use the Web!** B. I. (Before Internet), spreading information had large costs: printing, travel, entertaining, and long-distance telephone charges. Circa 1998, the Web has reduced these costs and made information available around the world.

- **Get all levels involved.** Information spreading, like pressing flesh, needs to be democratized and institutionalized. Enable all parts of your company to share in their special knowledge whether the function is research or copyright law.

It may seem like an odd metaphor but by now I hope you understand why eating like a bird and pooping like an elephant is a serious and powerful technique to catalyze revolutionary change!

One final example: Stan Lee, the chairman of Marvel Comics and Marvel Films, and John Buscema, the comic book legend whose characters include Silver Surfer and Conan, collaborated on a book called *How to Draw Comics the Marvel Way*. Marvel also released the first issue of a new comic book on the Internet prior to publishing and found that this seemingly suicidal act increased sales of the printed version.[18]

What open acts of courage! Marvel was saying, "This is how to copy our style" and "Download this comic book for free."

Readings for Revolutionaries

The Intelligence Edge: How to Profit in the Information Age, George Friedman, Meredith Friedman, Colin Chapman, and John S. Baker Jr., Crown Publishers, 1997, ISBN: 0609600753.

Managing the Flow of Technology, Thomas J. Allen, MIT Press, 1984, ISBN: 0262510278.

8

Think Digital, Act Analog

Create like a god, screw up like a man, grovel like a dog.

Peter N. Glaskowsky

Use Technology as a Tool . . .

Thinking digital means using technology to look at real data, track interactions with customers, and mine for information to serve people better. It requires thinking clearly and precisely rather than relying on hearsay, habits, and prejudices.

Acting analog means using a personal touch. No revolution ever succeeded without a high degree of analog contact—no matter how great your product, how leveraged your marketing, or how cool your Web site. When all is browsed, e-mailed, voice-mailed, and faxed, it's still an analog world.

The Ritz-Carlton Hotel Company* is one of the best examples of using technology to act analog. It has recorded more than 500,000 individual customer requests and preferences in a database system. Once information such as pillow preferences is recorded, guest recognition representatives at all Ritz-Carlton locations can access and act on it.

The collection of this data is an analog process: "There's an art behind how we do it," says Nadia Kyzer, corporate manager,

---

*<http://www.ritzcarlton.com/>

guest recognition. "We don't ask right out what customers want." It's up to the guest recognition coordinators to chat casually with guests and continually inform staffers of their preferences—especially for the chain's most frequent visitors.

What's especially important is that Ritz-Carlton uses the power of digital technology to enhance, not supplant, a personal relationship. Similarly, Peapod Inc., the online grocery shopping service, knows which items customers usually buy and presents them with this personal information to speed the shopping process. Digital technology—computers, databases, and networks—makes this possible.

(I love hotel examples. Here's another instance of good analog behavior: the Little Nell Hotel in Aspen, Colorado. Its concierges call guests at least two weeks before they arrive in order to answer questions, make restaurant reservations, and arrange for transportation.[1] This is acting analog!)

. . . But Use Technology Carefully

Great as it can be, digital technology can also create negative feelings by invading people's privacy or simply being a pain in the ass. I hate it, for example, when I buy a $2 battery at Radio Shack, and the clerk asks my name and address so that Radio Shack can do "relationship marketing" with me.

Digital power is easy to abuse, so keep these two principles in mind when you're thinking digital (the next chapter, "Don't Ask People to Do Something That You Wouldn't" covers this general topic in greater detail).

First, never *require* customers to give you personal information. The information might be crucial for your database and direct marketing efforts, but that's your problem, not your customers'. Has a sales clerk at Nordstrom (the most analog of retailers) ever asked for your name and address?

The best kind of data collection is done without intervention at all. When I visit Amazon.com's Web site, the company suggests books for me to purchase by reviewing my account history. By contrast, I've been flying on United Airlines for years (at the rate of about 100,000 miles), and every time I call, I still have to ask for an aisle seat and a fruit platter.

Second, use the information judiciously. If your customers are willing to give you this information, use it but use it judiciously. That is, don't inundate them with marketing and sales crap.

Third, don't collect information if you're not going to do something with it. Bombarding customers with useless advertisements, in fact, maybe be less heinous than collecting scads of information just so you can "have it on hand."

Ideally, you and your customers should both derive value from the information they provide. Short of this, at least your customers should get some value. But if it's only you that derives value, then you're hassling your customers for insufficient reason. Being a customer of your company should never entail the burden of being mere data for your research projects.

EXERCISE

If Ritz-Carlton started an airline, would you fly on it?

Extra credit: Would this airline ask you twice what type of seat and food you'd like?

Identify the Right Decision-Makers

Revolutionaries often make three key mistakes at the start of a revolution when they start marketing and evangelizing their product:

First, thinking that someone can make a decision when they can't. In 1983 and 1984 Apple came up with a typical yuppie, yellow-paisley-tie-MBA, digital analysis:

> Macintosh is a business computer, and businesses look up to *Fortune* 500 companies. *Fortune* 500 companies are run by presidents, vice-presidents, and MIS directors. These folks have the titles, therefore they have the power. Let's sell them on Macintosh, and they will make top-down decisions to put Macintoshes in their companies.

This strategy sold five Macintoshes. The executives, by and large, either couldn't make the decision or didn't want to. They had other things to worry about and focusing on them was a mistake.

Second, thinking that someone can't make a decision when they can. In the lower and bottom parts of *Fortune* 500 companies, at all levels of *Fortune* 5,000,000 companies, and throughout educational institutions, the salt of the earth—students, teachers, artists, designers, interns, consultants, and writers—were loving Macintosh.

These folks were the right decision-makers for Apple because they did the work, so they were the first to see how the Macintosh revolution could help them. They became Apple's evangelists and made Macintosh successful. However, if you just looked at their place on organization charts, you would have thought they couldn't help.

EXERCISE

When you don't know what to do about a problem, whom do you ask?

   A. Your spouse.

   B. Your secretary.

   C. Your shrink.

   D. Your inner child.

Third, assuming that there is only one decision-maker. Preserved Treescapes of Oceanside, California, sells artificial and preserved plants and trees for interior landscapes. Landscape architects who design the interiors for commercial real estate were live-tree snobs and would not talk to president and CEO Dennis Gabrick, so his first customers were landscape contractors—the people in charge of caring for plants in a hotel or shopping mall.

"It was that person's fault when something went wrong," says Gabrick. "I know that one third of all live plants will die each year. I had a way to give them preserved or artificial plants that last ten years or more. When we first started, we got these types of mid-range projects with people just trying to save monthly operational dollars."

Once these contractors started using preserved plants, the idea became accepted, and landscape architects began considering Gabrick's service. Gabrick knew he could save a building owner or developer the major expense of accommodating live plants, but instead of targeting them directly, he focused on the landscape architects who had a lot to gain by taking credit for saving money on a project.

Identifying the right decision-makers is an analog process. There usually isn't a single person who can make a unilateral yes/no decision. Instead there are usually several people who can help your revolution, and they, in turn, are influenced by many others.

Ignore People's Titles

As the Macintosh introduction experience showed, one of the biggest barriers to identifying the decision-maker is paying too much attention to people's titles.

Here's a nonbusiness story to illustrate the concept. One of the subscribers to the Rules for Revolutionaries Internet mailing list found himself deposited in front of twenty-two Siberian Yupik seventh and eighth graders in an Eskimo village in rural Alaska. In an Eskimo village, the climate and living conditions are so harsh that teacher turnover is often 100 percent per year. To the locals, school staff is often little more than an ever-changing parade of clowns.

The teacher realized that his Eskimo aide was the one constant in his student's educational lives. Instead of telling the aide what to do, this teacher picked his brain and the brains of the entire nonteaching staff. Teaching is a fairly hierarchical profession, so it's unusual to seek the counsel of those below you on the ladder, especially when they might not have even a high school education and they speak broken English.

In this case, these very people saved him from many mistakes, however, and established the tone of his relationship with parents all around the village. His students were mysteriously better behaved. The word got out that he was respectful of them because he ignored the humble titles of the "aides" during the first few weeks of school, so they became more respectful of him.[2]

Highfalutin titles don't mean a person is knowledgeable and powerful, and humble titles don't mean a person is dumb and powerless. Big titles mean little to a revolutionary. All you care is about is that a person "gets it" and wants to help you.

Ignoring people's titles also means ignoring the titles of your own employees. That is, don't limit personal contact to employees who usually work with customers—instead, let the whole company in on the fun. You will impress customers if employees of all kinds, not just the ones whose job is "customer service," are helping them. And employees will learn more about customers and better serve them.

In *Best Practices*, Robert Hiebler, Thomas Kelly, and Charles Ketteman discuss a United Airlines* employee named Patricia O'Brien Saari. Saari is an account executive in United's Seattle office, and she started a volunteer program called "100,000 Miles of Thanks." Employees in various positions wrote to 100,000-mile frequent flyers thanking them for their business and reminding them to take advantage of the special perks of 100,000-mile flyers.[3]

This is a beautiful illustration of thinking digital and acting analog: United's computers tracked their most frequent flyers, but United's employees took the analog step of sending them letters which increased their loyalty to the airline.

Show Up in Person

> You can dream, create, design, and build the most beautiful place in the world, but it requires people to make it reality.[4]
>
> *Walt Disney*

---

* <http://www.ual.com/>

This rule is in the category of "do as I say, not as I do" because my preferred means of communication, in descending order of preference, is e-mail, fax, telephone, letter, and face-to-face meeting.

Mea culpa—e-mails, faxes, and phone calls (particularly voice-mail messages) are not as effective as showing up in person. Thus, the good news is that showing up in person has become a powerful technique for revolutionaries because few people take the time and effort to do so. Showing up in person develops closer relationships with your customers. This means that they will provide more ideas for how to improve your product or service, be more tolerant of your mistakes, and will be less likely to switch vendors over price differences.*

The point is that simply showing up in person is a powerful sales and evangelism technique, so get out of your chair and get into your car or on an airplane to optimize results. Use e-mail, faxes, and voice mail as second-string methods to get personal.

Also, not only is the pen mightier than the sword, it is also mightier than the word processor and e-mail client. If you can't get to your customer in person or after you have met in person, use the simplest, cheapest, and mightiest ways to get personal: handwritten notes on elegant stationary.

Hang with the Hoi Polloi

For the longest time, I thought that hoi polloi referred to the elite, upper crust of people (after all, it is a foreign and therefore hoity-toity sounding word). It refers to exactly the opposite: the common people. It's not enough to show up in person. You have to hang out with the right people. This recommenda-

---

*People are also less likely to enforce piddly rules on you in person. For example, airlines have all sorts of rules about what it costs to change flight reservations, who can get upgraded to first class, and what coupons can be used. Next time, instead of trying to convince a reservationist on the phone to bend the rules for you, go to the airline's ticket office during a time when it's not busy and make your request in person.

tion is a step beyond ignoring titles because it involves intentionally communicating with Joe Sixpack as an ongoing practice. Here's why:

- **You'll get faster access to people in the future.** Secretaries, receptionists, administrative aides, and spouses control the world. (Behind every successful executive stands an amazed secretary.) These folks control access to The Boss, and there will be a time you will need access to The Boss, so be nice before you need a connection.

- **It's good for the morale.** Just before dawn one day at Disneyland, some maintenance workers were surprised to see Walt himself, in pajamas and bathrobe, padding down Main Street U.S.A. (He had a private apartment above the Firehouse, where he often spent the night.) "Come on," he said. "I know where the key to the orange juice dispenser is." And off they went to the Sunkist juice bar for a little morale building.[5]

- **The support staff knows how to work the system.** A school district in Florida had an approved vendor list from which departments could buy equipment. An unapproved but popular vendor was informed by the hoi polloi that "upgrades" are not subject to this restriction. He did a boatload of computer business as a result.

- **You'll get the real scoop.** In his book *What Do You Care What Other People Think?*, Richard Feynman explains the now famous story of how he conducted *his* investigation of the Challenger explosion. He met with the engineers who worked on the shuttle while the rest of the committee investigating the incident was spoon-fed sanitized, cover-your-ass information by managers.

- **It can save your butt.** A member of the Rules for Revolutionaries Internet mailing list sent me this e-mail to explain how hanging with the hoi polloi kept him out of trouble. I reprint it here complete with spelling mistakes—truer words were never spoken!

I am a senior in highschool. Early on, I befrended the office secritaries. Over the course of the past 4 years, I've gotten out of 36 suspensions and countless detentions. Beaurocrats are the ones with the real power.[6]

Catalyze a Virtual Community

Although the Ritz-Carlton uses digital technology to personalize its service for guests, the hotel is always the hub of activity and its guests the spokes. The guests seldom interact with each other when compared to other groups such as Saturn,* Macintosh, or Harley-Davidson† owners.

You too can build a community of people interested in your revolution by supporting the creation of such "user groups." These are organizations made up of people who share a common interest. You can use technology to assist in this analog process by building a virtual community on the Internet.

Many companies think that building a virtual community is as simple as throwing up a cool Web site that compels people to visit every day. Dream on. These sites are commercials, not communities. If you want to build a virtual community, here are the principles to implement:

- **Community before commerce.** In the words of John Hagel III and Arthur G. Armstrong (authors of *Net.Gain*), "put community before commerce."[7] That is, the purpose of these efforts is to build a community, not sell more stuff, so cool it on the commercialism. The community exists for its own benefit, not yours.

- **Communication comes next.** Build in the capability for people to communicate with each other via message boards and Internet mail lists. Peer-to-peer communication is more important than being able to communicate with the com-

---

*<http://www.saturn.com/>

†<http://www.harley-davidson.com/>

pany. You're hosting the event, but it's a cocktail party, not a lecture.

- **Place the community's interests above your own.** The big picture is that a vibrant community will help you, but getting to this place means sacrificing short-term interests. For example, people should be able to freely discuss and endorse competitive products.

- **Tolerate criticism.** Not only should people feel free to plug competitive products, they should be able to criticize your own. This freedom produces two desirable results: first, good public relations because tolerating criticism on a company-sponsored site is unheard of; second, free and voluminous customer feedback.

- **Encourage "personalities."** Remember how one of the keys to the success of MTV was veejays with an attitude? The same is true of a Web site, so encourage your employees to develop online personalities to show that corporate thought police don't control your site.

A great example of a company that has built a virtual community is Motley Fool.* Two fools, Tom and Dave Gardner, founded the company in 1994 to proselytize the concept of taking personal control of one's investments. If you visit its Web site, you'll see a very cohesive community that focuses on peer-to-peer investment advice.

Collaborate for Customer Share

Collaborative marketing occurs when you listen as the customer speaks, and when you invite a customer to participate in actually making the product.

Don Peppers and Martha Rogers

---

*<http://www.fool.com/>

In their book *The One to One Future: Building Relationships One Customer at a Time*, Don Peppers and Martha Rogers evangelize the concept of share of customer instead of share of market. Share of market takes this approach: If we could just sell one can of soda to every person in China ... Peppers and Rogers's approach is not acquiring market share, but capturing the lion's share of customers' ongoing, lifetime business.

The way to get customer share is to collaborate with them. According to *Webster's New World Dictionary*, "collaborate" means, "To work together, especially in some literary, artistic, or scientific undertaking."* Collaboration is the purest form of getting personal because you've not only found the right people, you're working with them for mutual benefit.

Peppers and Rogers offer seven tips to foster collaboration with customers:

- **Stop referring to them with militaristic and adversarial terms.** These terms include "target," "segment," and "wars." How about simply "people" or "customers"?

- **Ensure that you have a high-quality product or service.** This type of product or service is a prerequisite to be considered worthy of collaboration by customers.

- **Focus on individuals.** Collaboration means the largest segment you're dealing with is one person—not entire populations or large groups.

- **Maintain a record of all transactions.** It's tough to collaborate when you don't know what that customer has bought from you. You may have millions of transactions, but each customer only remembers his own.

- **Find and eliminate anything that hinders a customer's happy patronage.** Your product or service doesn't have to

---

Nota bene: the second definition in *Webster's* is "to cooperate with an enemy invader." This definition is not recommended.

be perfect, but you have to be willing to improve it. To do this, you have to know what the hindrances were in the first place.

- **Use complaints as a means to garner more business.** My first boss, Marty Gruber, taught me a valuable lesson: As long as customers are still complaining, they still want to do business. When they stop complaining, that's when you have to start worrying.

- **Create ways for customers to collaborate with you.** Just as I believe that every product can be evangelized, Peppers and Rogers probably believe that every product can lead to collaboration if you want collaboration to occur.

EXERCISE

Guy's Mensch Aptitude Test (GMAT) *

The word that best describes the highest form of good analog behavior: mensch. It is a Yiddish word that connotes a person who is admired, respected, and trusted because of a sense of ethics, fairness, and nobility.

For example:

The score is ten to ten in a pickup basketball game in which the first team to score eleven points wins. There are more than enough people waiting for the next game, so whatever team loses has to sit. A woman double dribbles, but no one sees her do it. Still, she calls the infraction on herself and gives the ball to the other team. She's a mensch.

An author is writing a business book and finds a concept in

---

*My source for the idea of a mensch quotient test is *The Secrets of Savvy Networking* by schmooze goddess Susan RoAne.

another book—say, the role of mensch-ness in business. While he isn't lifting any text from the book or using anything except the core of the idea itself, he cites the author because he believes she should get the credit due her. He's a mensch.

A diamond buyer working for a large, successful jewelry retailer places an order with a small, startup jewelry designer. The buyer knows that the startup is dying to do business with the retailer and would extend it long payment terms just to get the business. But the buyer doesn't press his advantage and pays the startup's invoices on time. The buyer is a mensch.

In business (and in life), a revolutionary who is a mensch has a great advantage because it's much easier to believe someone you admire. This chapter ends with the GMAT, so that you can determine your Mensch Quotient (MQ).

Do you help people even if you don't need something from them?

> Often (10 points).
>
> Sometimes (5 points).
>
> Never (0 points).

Do you pay back your markers?

> Always (10 points).
>
> Sometimes (5 points).
>
> Never (0 points).
>
> What's a marker? (–5 points)

Do you try to make the spouses of business associates feel comfortable at social gatherings?

> Always (10 points).
>
> Sometimes (5 points).

Never (0 points).

What's a spouse? (–10 points).

How often do you send handwritten notes to people?

Five or more times per week (10 points).

One to four times per week (5 points).

Never (0 points).

How fast do you answer correspondence (letter, fax, or e-mail)?

One hour (15 points).

One day (10 points).

One week (5 points).

One year (–5 points).

"A secretary is just a barrier between me and the person I want to get to."

Disagree (10 points).

Agree (0 points).

What's a secretary? (–5 points)

Scoring

60–65 points	A mensch's mensch. Leo Rosten should cite you as an example in the next edition of *The Joys of Yiddish*.
45–60 points	Still a chance to achieve menschdom if you don't hang around MBAs.
25–45 points	Go sell used cars.
0–25 points	Go sell broken used cars.

Readings for Revolutionaries

Net.Gain—Expanding Markets Through Virtual Communities, John Hagel III and Arthur G. Armstrong, Harvard Business School Press, 1997, ISBN: 0875847595.

The One to One Future: Building Relationships One Customer at a Time, Don Peppers and Martha Rogers, Currency/Doubleday, 1997, ISBN: 0385485662.

The Secrets of Savvy Networking: How to Make the Best Connections for Business and Personal Success, Susan RoAne, Warner Books, 1993, ISBN: 0446394106.

Turned On—Eight Vital Insights to Energize Your People, Customers, and Profits, Roger Dow and Susan Cook, HarperBusiness, 1997, ISBN: 0887308619.

9

Don't Ask People to Do Something That You Wouldn't

I have the simplest of taste. I'm easily satisfied with the best.

Oscar Wilde

The $110,000 Lesson

Five years ago I invested $110,000 in a software company. Its product was a high-end application that combined the functionality of a spreadsheet with a database. When the company went out of business, I lost every penny that I invested.

I served on the company's board of directors, so I had a front-row seat when big decisions were made. One of my more vivid memories was a board meeting at which the vice-president of sales explained these points: (1) There were 1,100 beta sites; (2) they all loved the product; and (3) he expected to have confirmed purchase orders or advance payments a month before final shipment (at the time he made this claim, it was six months before the projected ship date).

I remember asking him why companies would commit to a product that hadn't shipped. He and the president of the company responded that I didn't understand the "enterprise market" (because my background was in consumer software) and that the company's product was so revolutionary that customers would make this commitment.

In fact, the potential customers did not issue purchase orders or make advance payments, and the software was late. Besides that, everything was fine. Of course, the company soon went out of business because it ran out of cash, and the venture capital investors refused to provide more money. So endeth the revolution.

My $110,000 was not altogether wasted, however. For that dear price I learned an important lesson:

Never ask your customer to do something that you wouldn't. *

There isn't a company on the planet that would commit a purchase order or advance payment to a piece of personal computer software. If we were looking for accounting software for the company, we would not have issued a purchase order or

---

*Actually, I learned three lessons but only the first is genuinely relevant to revolutionaries. I'll throw in the other two, though, so that I feel like my money was well wasted:

- **Caveat director.** When you're in a position of power and responsibility like an executive or board member, you shouldn't go with the flow when you see something that blatantly violates common sense. You should argue against it—and you should keep arguing against it—until you either are convinced you're wrong or you convert the others to your perspective.

- **Unless a software company is within eight weeks of shipping a product, the company has no idea of the actual date.** Here's what a software company is really saying when it offers these typical answers to the question, What stage is the software in? "Feature complete"—twelve months to shipping; "optimizing performance"—six months to shipping; "our beta sites love the product"—the venture capitalists will never get their money back; "we don't release this information"—the product is being rewritten from scratch; and "within thirty to sixty days"—before the next shareholders' meeting.

paid in advance, and yet we were asking our customers to do just that.

Other People's Lessons

Not everyone has to spend $110,000 for his own personal examples of this lesson—you're getting three for the price of this book. Here are two others, in different fields, that cost only an enormous amount of frustration.

First, a California bank used computers to call people at home in the evening. If the phone was answered, the computer asked the person to hold until a sales representative came on the line![1]

What got into the brain of the bank's marketing honcho? Going from home banking (which was a revolutionary idea) to *hold* banking isn't progress. Surely the executives of the bank would not tolerate calls like this at their homes from other companies, and yet they expected their customers to put up with it.

EXERCISE

The next time a telemarketer calls you at home, ask for his phone number and tell him that you'll call him at home that night.

Second, an example of "have it our way" service. Michele Moreno, my research assistant, had problems with her AT&T* cordless phone, so she called the AT&T warranty division. This is what she went through:

• First she listened to an introduction explaining that the AT&T warranty division had changed its name to Lucent Technologies.

---
*<http://www.att.com/>

- Then she had to choose from three different departments.

- Then she had to choose from four different options for service.

- Then she had to choose from several types of products.

- Then she had to enter a model number.

- Then she had to choose from a list of seven common types of problems.

- She pressed the appropriate number for her problem and was given four steps to try after she hung up the phone.

- Then the recording stated "If you have followed these, and your phone is still not working, please redial the 800 number again and press *7 for assistance."

I'm all for throwing technology like voice mail at problems, but forcing customers through this type of labyrinth is unreasonable. AT&T is screaming at its customers, "Have it our way!"

EXERCISE

If your company has voice mail, call it and see if it is better than AT&T's.

Get Over the Paranoia

The story may be apocryphal, but Nordstrom supposedly allowed a customer to return an automobile tire that he insisted he bought at the store. Of course, Nordstrom doesn't sell tires.

The paranoid would ask, "But what if everyone who owns a car returned tires to Nordstrom? Nordstrom would go broke!" But people won't (and don't), and Nordstrom will never be in danger of going bankrupt for accepting returns of goods it doesn't sell.

Managers are afraid to implement customer-pleasing, revolution-catalyzing policies because they are afraid that too many people will take advantage of these policies, and they'll end up with the equivalent of a store full of tires.

Empower Your Employees

Empowered employees are empathetic employees. Given the freedom and support, they would do the right things in the right way for customers. It's when "management" gets involved—setting goals, establishing standards, and injecting spreadsheet-based fear—that things go awry.

For example, employees of the Ritz-Carlton (there are 14,000 of them) are empowered to spend up to $2,000 to fix a guest's problem with the hotel—not just management-level employees, but any employee: maid, bellhop, or doorman.[2]

If every employee spent $2,000 on just one customer then the Ritz-Carlton would probably go broke (14,000 × $2,000 = $28,000,000), but it's also true that employees aren't so stupid and guests aren't so dishonest that this would happen.

Empowered employees are profit and customer-loyalty gen-erating ones. A friend of mine was once frustrated by an airline employee's unwillingness and inability to rectify an accounting issue, so he walked over to the Southwest Airlines counter and explained the situation.

The Southwest Airlines* employee matched the price of the other airline's thirty-days-in-advance fare by pretending that my friend had purchased the ticket seven days in advance. Southwest Airlines got $250 worth of business that it wouldn't have gotten and a loyal customer because of this act of an empowered employee.

This decision was an empowered, nonparanoid, and highly "analog" decision. The policy was such and such, but the employee did what was right for the customer.

---

*<http://www.southwest.com/>

Put Customers in Control

The flip side to empowered employees is empowered customers. When customers feel as if they have no power, they react negatively and strongly. (And, as mentioned in Chapter 1, the feeling of powerlessness in people is the sign of a market opportunity.)

For example, an airline loses your luggage and then tells you its policy is to wait forty-eight hours to see if it is found. *Then* you can buy a toothbrush and the airline will reimburse your expenses. Whose fault was it that the luggage was lost anyway? And would the airline personnel not brush their teeth for forty-eight hours?

The more effective method is to put the customers in control. This is a two-step process: First, give them accurate and truthful information. For example, United Parcel Service* enables its customers to track the location of packages anywhere in the world by entering a tracking number or sending an e-mail to a server with the tracking number as the subject of the message.

Second, let customers decide what they want to do. The vast majority of people are reasonable, so let your empowered employees take care of your empowered customers. You'll also find that when people feel as if they have power, they will often forgive the slip-ups and mishaps that inevitably occur.

Underpromise and Overdeliver

The only aspect of this recommendation that is more astounding than its simplicity is the rarity with which you find it implemented. Take this as gospel: Make announcements that you know you can achieve and then strive to do better. Many a revolution never got started because it was overhyped.

Does this mean you should sandbag people? Absolutely. When you meet your commitments (which is the least you

---

*<http://www.ups.com/>

should do), people will be pleasantly surprised. When you exceed your commitments, people will be astounded. If you do nothing but fulfill your announcements, you might be considered a revolutionary for this reason alone.

Exercise

True or false?

There are signs along the waiting lines for the rides at Disneyland and Disney World. These signs indicate the length of time you have to wait to get on a ride from that point. These signs are purposely overstated.

Treat Your Customers Like *Kamaainas*

If you've traveled to Hawaii, you may have noticed *kamaaina* prices for airlines, hotels, and most tourist attractions. These prices are from 20 percent to 30 percent lower than the price for everyone else. *Kamaaina* is the Hawaiian word for "local." In practice, it refers to people who are citizens of Hawaii no matter where they came from originally. (In my case, though I lived in Hawaii for twenty years, I'm now a California resident, so I pay the same price as tourists.)

Businesses support *kamaaina* pricing because *kamaainas* are existing, long-term, and repeat customers and because it's good public relations to support members of the local community. By contrast, because most companies want to attract new business (there's the market share death magnet again!) they end up treating their current customers worse than new customers or customers of their competition. Here are two examples of treating customers like tourists.

First, a high-end magazine for audio enthusiasts created a CD of high-quality recordings. If you were a new subscriber to the magazine, you got this CD as a gift. If you were a current subscriber, you had to pay $17.[3] In fact, many magazines offer new subscriptions for less than renewable ones. As a subscriber, why shouldn't I stop my subscription and restart it later or defect to a competitor?

Second, many cellular phone service providers offer new phones for free in exchange for signing up with them. However, if you were an existing customer, you'd have to pay the full price for the same phone. Naturally, many customers simply switch service providers—becoming a "new" customer for another company.[4]

Think Allocentrically

So far this chapter has been about avoiding negative results by not asking customers to do something bad, silly, inconvenient, or just plain stupid that you wouldn't do. However, if your competition is asking people to do something suboptimal, then it's creating an opportunity for you. All you have to do is think allocentrically.

Adam M. Brandenburger and Barry J. Nalebuff explain thinking allocentrically in their book *Co-opetition*. It means putting yourself in the place of a different type of person—to face problems as another type of person.[5]

For example, a Whirlpool employee taped a news program's interview with Gail, a woman with several children and a full-time job. Whirlpool employees were challenged to provide appliances that would "take care of Gail." In response, they redesigned the stovetop of Whirlpool's CleanTop to be completely flat, without grease traps or dirt-collecting crevices, and they created the Quiet Partner dishwasher, so the noise of the dishwasher wouldn't distract Gail. Viewing chores through Gail's eyes has helped Whirlpool introduce significant product enhancements.

Here are more inspiring examples of allocentric thinking:

- **Senior citizens.** At Children's Wonderland, a daycare facility in Oxnard, California, most of the attendees are children under six years old, but there are also fifteen senior citizens who are suffering from frailty or dementia. At this facility, senior citizens do not face the usual boredom and isolation of a seniors-only facility. Instead, they can play with children.[6] You wouldn't want to be bored all day, so don't ask senior citizens to be either.

- **Pregnant women.** Mark and Matt Emerson are twenty-seven-year-old twins and the founders of Maternal Concepts.* They are both single, and neither has kids. However, thinking allocentrically, they've created the Prenatal Baby Cradle maternity mattress. It is a baby-blue air mattress with two holes in it: one is the "breast chamber" and the other is the "abdomen chamber." The goal is to enable pregnant women to sleep on their stomachs. You can rent a mattress for $157 for three months or buy it for $249.95 if more kids are in the plan.[7]

EXERCISE

(For men only.) Strap a twenty-five pound weight to your stomach for nine months. See if you're not cranky.

- **Disabled.** Designers at the Ontario Rehabilitation Technology Consortium† developed a toilet seat for children with cerebral palsy by putting themselves in the position of the user and the caregiver. Other products on the market use straps and buckles to fasten the child into place—leading to a scary-looking device and a less than comfortable user. The Consortium designers focused on a positioning system that enhances stability, making any straps or fasteners unnecessary. The unit is also far easier for the caregiver to handle and is appealing to both children with cerebral palsy and their able-bodied siblings.[8]

---

*<http://www.maternalconcepts.com/>

†<http://www.oise.utoronto.ca>

- **Korean.** Kimchi is a spiced, pickled cabbage Korean dish with a very potent smell. As it ages, it produces gases that would pop the top off most containers. Thinking Korean, Tupperware* designed a product called Kimchi Keeper. The seal of this large container has a soft dome that will pop up as gas is released from the cabbage. A vent in the seal can be opened to release the gas emitted by the kimchi. The bottom of each container has a rise to allow for stacking.

Be Cool

I end this chapter with a story that was sent to me via the Rules for Revolutionaries Internet mailing list that illustrates the power of not asking people to do something you wouldn't.

A small, newly created bank in Sri Lanka was struggling to find a niche for itself in a crowded market.[9] The chairman of the bank took a consultant to his branches and the competition's. The weather was very hot and humid, and the air was polluted. Later that day, after a very good lunch in an air-conditioned, five-star hotel, they returned to his air-conditioned office.

The consultant noticed that none of the banks—his client's or the competition's—was air-conditioned. They were all "shop houses" with iron doors and grills that are removed in the morning and replaced at the end of the day. His recommendation to the client was simple: Air-condition your banks.

The bank credits part of its successful start to the air-conditioning, and management still air-conditions all the branches, no matter how remote the location, because they wouldn't want to bank in a hot, stuffy, polluted atmosphere.

The smallest things can get your revolution rolling or stop it dead in its tracks. You are a lot more likely to achieve the former if you always put yourself in the shoes of your customers.

---

*<http://www.tupperware.com/>

EXERCISE

Which of the following effects did the invention of air-conditioning have?[10]

    A. Larger bureaucracies in the federal government.

    B. Better movie-going experiences.

    C. The isolation of neighbors in Southern states.

    D. The creation of Las Vegas.

    E. All of the above.

Readings for Revolutionaries

Marketing High Technology—An Insider's View, William H. Davidow, Free Press, 1986, ISBN: 002907990X.

PART 4

CONCLUSION

10

Don't Let Bozosity Grind You Down (*Ne Te Terant Molarii**)

Technology and Inventions

[W]hen the Paris Exhibition closes electric light will close with it and no more will be heard of it.

Erasmus Wilson, professor at Oxford University,[†] *1878*

Well-informed people know it is impossible to transmit the voice over wires and that were it possible to do so, the thing would be of no practical value.

Editorial in the Boston Post, *1865*

---

*The literal translation of this Latin phrase is, "Don't let the plodding millers grind you down." Courtesy of Nina Barclay (via Holly Camerota) of the Norwich Free Academy.

[†]<http://www.ox.ac.uk/>

This "telephone" has too many shortcomings to be seriously considered as a means of communication. The device is inherently of no value to us.

Western Union* internal memo, 1876

You could put in this room, DeForest, all the radiotelephone apparatus that the country will ever need.

W. W. Dean, president of the Dean Telephone Company, to Lee DeForest, the American radio pioneer, 1907

While theoretically and technically television may be feasible, commercially and financially I consider it an impossibility, a development of which we need waste little time dreaming.

Lee DeForest, quoted in the New York Times,† *1926*

[Man will never reach the moon] regardless of all future scientific advances.

Lee DeForest, inventor of the audion tube, New York Times, *February 25, 1957*

I am tired of this thing called science. . . . We have spent millions in that sort of thing for the last few years, and it is time it should be stopped.

Simon Cameron, U.S. senator from Pennsylvania, demanding that funding end for the Smithsonian Institution,‡ 1861

---

* <http://www.westernunion.com/>

† <http://www.nyt.com/>

‡ <http://www.si.edu/>

Everything that can be invented has been invented.

Charles H. Duell, Commissioner,
U.S. Office of Patents,* 1899

Computers

I think there is a world market for about five computers.

Remark attributed to Thomas Watson,
chairman of the board of IBM, 1943

I have traveled the length and breadth of this country and talked with the best people in business administration. I can assure you on the highest authority that data processing is a fad and won't last out the year.

The editor in charge of business books at
Prentice-Hall,† responding to Karl V. Karstrom
(a junior editor who recommended a
manuscript about data processing), circa 1957

There is no reason for any individual to have a computer in their home.

Ken Olsen, president of Digital
Equipment Corporation,‡ at the Convention of the
World Future Society, 1977

So we went to Atari and said, "Hey, we've got this amazing thing, even built with some of your parts, and what do you think about funding us? Or we'll give it to you. We just want to do it. Pay our salary, we'll come

---

* <http://www.uspto.gov/>

† <http://www.prenhall.com/>

‡ <http://www.dec.com/>

work for you." And they said, "No." So then we went to Hewlett-Packard, and they said, "Hey, we don't need you. You haven't got through college yet."

Apple Computer Inc. founder Steve Jobs on attempts to get Atari and H-P* interested in his and Steve Wozniak's personal computer

640K ought to be enough for anybody.

Bill Gates, 1981

Transportation

The ordinary "horseless carriage" is at present a luxury for the wealthy; and although its price will probably fall in the future, it will never, of course, come into as common use as the bicycle.

The Literary Digest, *October 14, 1899*

That the automobile has practically reached the limit of its development is suggested by the fact that during the past year no improvements of a radical nature have been introduced.

Scientific American,[†] *January 2, 1909*

Heavier-than-air flying machines are impossible.

Lord Kelvin, British mathematician, physicist, and president of the British Royal Society,[‡] circa 1895

---

* <http://www.hp.com/>

[†] <http://www.sciam.com/>

[‡] <http://www.royalsoc.ac.uk/>

[Airplanes] are interesting toys but of no military value.

Maréchal Ferdinand Foch, professor of strategy at and commandant of Supérieure de Guerre, 1911

Professor Goddard does not know the relation between action and reaction and the need to have something better than a vacuum against which to react. He seems to lack the basic knowledge ladled out daily in high schools.

1921 New York Times editorial about Robert Goddard's revolutionary rocket work

Political Revolution

The French people are incapable of regicide.

King Louis XVI of France, circa 1789, (he was convicted of treason and beheaded in 1793)

Your constitution is all sail and no anchor. . . . Either some Caesar or Napoleon will seize the reins of government with a strong hand; or your republic will be . . . laid waste by barbarians in the twentieth century as the Roman Empire was in the fifth.

Thomas Babington Macaulay, British statesman and author, 1857

New Businesses

C.

The grade Professor Challis A. Hall, Jr. gave to Fred Smith's term paper for Economics 43A in 1965. Smith went on to use the hub-and-spoke concept he wrote about in the paper to form Federal Express.[1]

A cookie store is a bad idea. Besides, the market research reports say America likes crispy cookies, not soft and chewy cookies like you make.

> *Response to Debbi Fields's idea of*
> *starting Mrs. Fields' Cookies**

Entertainment

The wireless music box has no imaginable commercial value. Who would pay for a message sent to nobody in particular?

> *David Sarnoff's associates in response to his urgings for*
> *investment in the radio in the 1920s*

Who'd pay to see a drawing of a fairy princess when they can watch Joan Crawford's boobs for the same price at the box office?

> *Louis B. Mayer referring to* Snow White

The cinema is little more than a fad. It's canned drama. What audiences really want to see is flesh and blood on the stage.

> *Charlie Chaplin, circa 1916*

Medical

[Louis Pasteur's] theory of germs is a ridiculous fiction.

> *Pierre Pachet, Professor of*
> *Physiology at Toulouse,*† *1872*

---

*<http://www.mrsfields.com/>

†<http://www.univ-tlse2.fr/>

The abdomen, the chest, and the brain will forever be shut from the intrusion of the wise and humane surgeon.

> *Sir John Eric Ericksen, British surgeon, appointed*
> *Surgeon-Extraordinary to Queen Victoria, 1837*

People

We do not believe in the permanence of his reputation.

> The Saturday Review, *London,*
> *May 8, 1858, on Charles Dickens*

I'm sorry, Mr. Kipling, but you just don't know how to use the English language.

> *Editor of the* San Francisco Examiner*
> *informing Rudyard Kipling (who had one*
> *article published) that he shouldn't submit a*
> *second article for publishing, 1889*

I'm just glad it'll be Clark Gable who's falling on his face and not Gary Cooper.

> *Gary Cooper on his decision not to take the leading*
> *role in* Gone with the Wind

Gauguin is . . . a decorator tainted with insanity.

> *Kenyon Cox, American painter and art critic,*
> Harper's Weekly, *March 15, 1913*

---

*<http://www.examiner.com/>

He couldn't hit an inside pitch to save his neck. If he were a white man I doubt if they would even consider him as big league material.

> *Bob Feller, Cleveland Indians pitcher, on the*
> *announcement that the Dodgers*
> *had signed Jackie Robinson, 1945*

It's too far to commute. And how can you make a business out of a search engine?

> *Guy Kawasaki, when asked if he would be interested in*
> *interviewing for the CEO position at Yahoo!*
> *when the company was starting*

Bozos Versus Bozosity

Initially, I called this chapter "Don't Let the Bozos Grind You Down," but when I reviewed the accomplishments of the people on the list (not to mention adding my own example), I realized that labeling someone a bozo because of one quote out of who-knows-what context is a bozo thing to do.

Very few people are total nincompoops. Sure, some guy said that telephones won't ever be useful and another gave the business plan for Federal Express a C, but these same people may have been terrific managers, raised wonderful children, inspired hundreds of students, and somehow made the world a better place. Are they necessarily bozos? I think not.*

That is why this chapter is about not letting *bozosity*, which can be a temporary affliction, grind you down. But before I dissect bozosity, I'd like to emphasize the need to resist being ground down. There is no better illustration of this point than the classic children's book *The Carrot Seed*. Here it is reprinted in full.

---

*On the other hand, if you enjoyed this collection of expertology, be sure to read *The Experts Speak* by Christopher Cerf and Victor Navasky. This book was my primary source for these quotes. It is the bible of bozosity.

And nothing came up.

Everyone kept saying it
wouldn't come up.

But he still pulled up the
weeds around it every day
and sprinkled the ground
with water.

Why Does Bozosity Exist?

Essentially, you can stop reading right here because *The Carrot Seed* says it all: Plant seeds, pull weeds, sprinkle feed, and believe. However, if you'd like to learn more about bozosity, please read on.

In *Inevitable Illusions*, Massimo Piattelli-Palmarini offers what he calls the Seven Deadly Sins that make people think they know something when they don't. These sins explain why bozosity exists, and knowing why it exists will help you defeat it.

- **Overconfidence.** The more knowledgeable someone is about a topic, the more overconfident and susceptible the person will be to blunders. This is why MIS people can be so wrong about computers.

EXERCISE

True or false? Potatoes originated in Peru.

- **Magical thinking.** When people are convinced of positive correlation, they will find additional confirmation and justify why the additional confirmation exists. By nature, people are confirmers and verifiers, not debunkers or contrarians.

- **Predictability in hindsight.** People often believe that they could have predicted what happened once they find out what happened. For example, once you hear that a product failed, you "knew" from the start that it would. Let's hear the prediction at the start, not after the fact.

- **Anchoring.** People remain anchored to their original opinions and have to be moved from these starting points. Thus, anchoring limits the practical range of opinions. When you think about most of the epigraphs cited at the front of this chapter, these people suffered most from an inability to see beyond the limits of their anchors.

- **Ease of representation.** The easier it is for people to envision how something happens, the more frequently they think it happens. For example, homicide is easy to imagine because of television shows and news reports, so people probably think it happens more frequently than suicide. But in reality, suicide claims more lives.

- **Probability blindness.** Most people have a poor understanding of probability. Piattelli-Palmarini's example is that people consider increasing the probability of winning a prize from 32 percent to 37 percent less desirable than increasing the probability from 94 percent to 99 percent. But 5 percent is 5 percent. This blindness is why state lotteries are so profitable.

- **Reconsideration under suitable scripts.** Mathematically, the occurrence of two events is always less likely than either event itself. However, people often link an improbable sequence of events to come up with a final outcome that seems more, not less, believable. For example, the United States invades Mexico, Mexico retaliates with a nuclear weapon provided by China, the United States attacks China, China attacks back, and the world ends.

Let's throw some of these sins at an imaginary hot, young entrepreneur with an idea for a revolutionary personal computer that defies the Windows hegemony.

An "expert" tells the entrepreneur that he will fail. This expert, formerly a product manager at a computer company, is now an industry analyst at International Data Corporation. Business publications frequently quote him. He tells the entrepreneur that she doesn't have a champagne-glass-in-a-toddler's-room chance of survival. (Overconfidence.)

He supports his statement and "proves" his expertise by saying, "I knew that Apple would be in trouble because it didn't support industry-standard operating systems from Microsoft." (Predictability in hindsight.)

After a short time, the entrepreneur achieves success. Certain niches of the market are quite pleased with the entrepreneur's new computer, but the expert still believes that she will never set a "platform standard" because of his initial prediction of failure. (Anchoring.)

The mainstream press shares this dim view of her chances. They easily envision the failure of a little startup computer company in its battle against all the giant companies selling Microsoft Windows machines. (Ease of representation.)

In their final, extremely bitter meeting, the expert tells the entrepreneur that this is why her company will certainly die:

- The new administration in Washington, D.C., is going to take a hands-off approach to business regulation.

- The Department of Justice will therefore free Microsoft to compete in any manner it sees fit.

- Microsoft will buy much of the press including newspapers and television networks. Thus, it can set and forever control all of the standards for information retrieval and delivery on the Internet.

- With nearly 100 percent market share and infinite resources, Microsoft will hire all of the talented college graduates in the world.

- After a decade, Microsoft will control the world. (Reconsideration under suitable scripts.)

Kick But

Life for a revolutionary is all about kicking but: "You have an interesting product, but . . . " "I can see where there needs to be a better way, but . . . " "I'd like to help you, but . . ." Here are the ways to defeat but-headed thinking:

- **Focus on customers, not schmexperts.** If you do what's right for your customers, eventually the experts, press, analysts, and naysayers will have to come around. If you do what's right for the experts, you may or may not be doing what's right for customers. But making experts happy is too risky. If you're not doing what's right for customers, you will most likely fail.

- **Ignore titles and trappings.**[2] Look for genuine proof of expertise, not externalities that are highly correlated with knowledge. Just because someone has an impressive title ("professor"), wears expensive clothes, and drives a nice car, doesn't mean you should listen to him. For that matter, just because someone doesn't have a title, wears jeans, and drives a beat-up car, doesn't mean you shouldn't listen to her.

- **Question authority.** Ask the question, "Is this person truly an expert?"[3] Then ask the question, "How truthful can you expect an expert to be?" The first question focuses your attention on what really matters—what people know—rather than the trappings mentioned above. The second question focuses your attention on the true and complete meaning of what an "expert" is telling you.

- **Listen and churn.** Elicit and then respond to the specific objections of naysayers, but stop short of believing that these objections mean your revolution will fail. Address these objections or decide that they are irrelevant and churn forward—a revolution is a process, not an event! Man will *never* fly? Why? . . . Engines can't generate enough power. Wings can't support enough weight. Controls can't keep the contraption stable. Then fix the engines, fix the wings, fix the controls, and fly—but don't succumb to the bozosity that "man will never fly."

- **Never consider the battle lost.** The battle is not lost if you live to fight another day. The battle can continue at another company or with another product or service. The battle is truly lost only when you surrender. For that matter, never consider the battle won. At the moment you consider the battle won, there are two guys in a garage, a gal and a guy in a garage, or two gals in a garage plotting the next revolution that will do to you what you did to the status quo.

MICROSOFT CORPORATION
10700 NORTHUP WAY
BELLEVUE, WASHINGTON 98004
206 828 8080 TLX: 328945

November 30, 1982

Mr. Guy Kawasaki
4543 Willis Avenue, #203
Sherman Oaks California 91403

Dear Mr. Kawasaki:

We appreciate your interest in Microsoft and welcomed the opportunity to review
your resume.

Your background has been reviewed against our current and anticipated staffing
requirements; however, we have been unable to identify a position that would
effectively utilize your capabilities at this time. We will retain your resume for
future consideration, up to six months, and if an appropriate opening develops,
contact you regarding your interest.

Thanks again for your interest in Microsoft, and best of luck to you in your career
search.

Sincerely,

Chris Grimes

Chris Grimes
Recruiter

CG:kjb

The battle is never lost—I did get into the software business!

- **Increase the level of truth.** In her book *Women's Reality—
  An Emerging Female System in a White Male Society,* Ann
  Wilson Schaef explains the concept of "levels of truth." It

means that people have attained different levels of understanding along a continuum, and whatever level they are at is their "truth." The challenge is that each successive level is usually at odds with the previous level. If you look at naysayers this way, your goal is to get them to the level where they understand the viability of your revolution.

- **Judge your results and other people's intentions.** This prevents you from judging people harshly because they "don't get it." Most people judge their own intentions and other people's results—which usually means they accept their own failings (because they had good intentions) but not the failings of others (because the results were lousy).

The Levels of Revolution

Don't worry about people stealing your ideas. If your ideas are any good, you'll have to ram them down people's throats.

Howard Aiken

My interpretation of naysaying, bozosity, and predictions of failure is that they indicate you're on to something. This doesn't mean that when people say your revolution will fail, it will necessarily succeed.

However, there is one certainty:

No matter what people say, if you don't try at all, you will never know.

So don't let anything grind you down: Create like a god, command like a king, and work like a slave. If you have revolutionary potential, then you have a moral imperative to make the world a better place.

You will find that defeating bozosity is more satisfying than accumulating trappings—and making the world a better place is more satisfying than defeating bozosity. Then you will understand the most important lesson of all:

The greatest role that life can bestow upon you is to be a revolutionary.

Readings for Revolutionaries

The Experts Speak—The Definitive Compendium of Authoritative Misinformation, Christopher Cerf and Victor Navasky, Pantheon Books, 1984, ISBN: 0394713346.

Inevitable Illusions—How Mistakes of Reason Rule Our Minds, Massimo Piattelli-Palmarini, John Wiley and Sons, 1996, ISBN: 047115962X.

List of Works Used

The ideas I stand for are not mine. I borrowed them from Socrates. I swiped them from Chesterfield. I stole them from Jesus. And I put them in a book. If you don't like their rules, whose would you use?

Dale Carnegie

Aaker, David A. "Should You Take Your Brand to Where the Action Is?" *Harvard Business Review* 75, no. 5 (1997): 135–143.

Aaker, David A. *Managing Brand Equity—Capitalizing on the Value of a Brand Name*. New York: The Free Press, 1991.

Adler Jr., Bill, and Julie Houghton. *America's Stupidest Business Decisions: 101 Blunders, Flops, and Screwups*. New York: William Morrow, 1997.

Alderson, Wroe. *Marketing Behavior and Executive Action*. Homewood, Illinois: Richard D. Irwin, 1957.

Allen, Oliver E. "Kettering." *Invention and Technology* 12 (Fall 1996): 52–63.

Allen, Thomas John. *Managing the Flow of Technology*. Cambridge: MIT Press, 1993.

Alley, James. "The Theory That Made Microsoft." *Fortune* (April 29, 1996): 65–66.

Anterasian, Cathy, John L. Graham, and R. Bruce Money. "Are U.S. Managers Superstitious about Market Share?" *Sloan Management Review* (Summer 1996): 67–77.

Bailey, Keith and Karen Leland. *Customer Service for Dummies*. Foster City: IDG Books Worldwide, Inc., 1995.

Barker, Joel Arthur. *Future Edge Paradigms: The Business of Discovering the Future*. New York: HarperBusiness, 1993.

Benjack, David J. and J. Michael MacKeen. "MTV Networks: MTV." *New Product Success Stories: Lessons from Leading Innovators*. New York: Wiley, 1995.

Benyus, Janine M. *Biomimicry: Innovation Inspired by Nature*. New York: William Morrow, 1997.

Brandenburger, Adam M. and Barry J. Nalebuff. *Co-opetition*. New York: Doubleday, 1996.

Brockman, John, and Katinka Matson, ed. *How Things Are: A Science Tool-Kit for the Mind*. New York: William Morrow, 1995.

Canfield, Jack et al. *Chicken Soup for the Soul at Work: 101 Stories of Courage, Compassion, and Creativity in the Workplace*. Deerfield Beach, Florida: Health Communications, 1996.

Cerf, Christopher and Victor Navasky, *The Expert's Speak*. New York: Pantheon Books, 1984.

Cialdini, Robert B. *Influence: The Psychology of Persuasion*. New York: William Morrow, 1984.

Clancy, Tom. *Into the Storm: A Study in Command*. New York: G. P. Putnam's Sons, 1997.

CNET Staff, "Gates: Why is Windows so cheap?" October 3, 1997. Web site.

D' Aveni, Richard A. *Hypercompetitive Rivalries: Competing in Highly Dynamic Environments*. New York: Free Press, 1995.

Davidow, William H. *Marketing High Technology*. New York: Collier Macmillan, 1986.

Donnelly, Kathleen. "Belly Down." *San Jose Mercury News,* 16 March 1997, *West* section: 7.

Dow, Roger and Susan Cook. *Turned On—Eight Vital Insights to Energize Your People, Customers, and Profits*. New York: HarperBusiness, 1996.

Downes, Larry and Chunka Mui. *Unleashing the Killer App— Digital Strategies for Market Dominance*. Boston: Harvard Business School Press, 1998.

Fishman, Mark C. et al. *Medicine,* 2nd ed. Philadelphia: J. B. Lippincott, 1985.

Flatow, Ira. *They All Laughed . . . from Lightbulbs to Lasers: The Fascinating Stories Behind the Great Inventions That Have Changed Our Lives.* New York: HarperCollins, 1992.

Freedman, David H. "The Butterfly Solution." *Discover,* April 1997: 53.

Friedel, Robert. "The Accidental Inventor. "*Discover,* October 1996: 58–69.

Friedman, George. *The Intellligence Edge: How to Profit in the Information Age,* New York: Crown Publishers, Inc., 1997.

Gardner, David, and Tom Gardner. *You Have More Than You Think: The Motley Fool Guide to Investing What You Have.* New York: Simon & Schuster, 1998.

Gelbert, Doug. *So Who the Heck Was Oscar Mayer?: The Real People Behind those Brand Names.* New York: Barricade Books, 1996.

Gersham, Michael. *Getting It Right The Second Time: How American Ingenuity Transformed Forty-Nine Marketing Failures Into Some Of Our Most Successful Products.* Reading, Mass: Addison-Wesley Publishing, 1990.

Goldsmith, Andrew. "Here's an Idea That's Not Quite Ripe." *Fast Company,* October-November 1997: 50.

Gould, Stephen Jay. "Creating the Creators." *Discover,* October 1996: 43–54.

Gubernick, Lisa. "Granny Care and Kiddie Care," *Forbes,* 30 December 1996: 74–75.

Hagel III, John and Arthur G. Armstrong. *Net.Gain—Expanding Markets Through Virtual Communications.* Boston: Harvard Business School Press, 1997.

Hamel, Gary. "Strategy as Revolution." *Harvard Business Review* 74, no. 4 (1996): 69–82.

Hendon, Donald W. *Classic Failures in Product Marketing: Marketing Principles Violations and How to Avoid Them.* New York: Quorum Books, 1992.

Henkoff, Ronald. "New Management Secrets from Japan—Really." *Fortune,* 27 November 1995.

Hiebler, Robert, Thomas Kelly, and Charles Ketteman. *Best Practices: Building Your Business with Customer-Focused Solutions*. New York: Simon & Schuster, 1998.

Huey, John. "Nothing is Impossible." *Fortune*, 23 September 1991.

Johansson, Johny K. and Ikujiro Nonaka. *Relentless*. New York: HarperCollins Publishers, 1996.

Johnson, Clarence L. *Kelly: More Than My Share of It All*. Washington D.C.: Smithsonian Institution Press, 1985.

Jones Jr., Malcolm. "Air Conditioning." *Newsweek Extra 2000*, Winter 1997–98: 42–43.

Kim, W. Chan and Renée Mauborgne, "Value Innovation: The Strategic Logic of High Growth." *Harvard Business Review* 75, no. 1 (1997): 103–112.

Krass, Peter. *The Book of Business Wisdom: Classic Writings by the Legends of Commerce and Industry*. New York: John Wiley & Sons, 1997.

Kriegel, Robert J. and David Brandt. *Sacred Cows Make the Best Burgers: Developing Change*. New York: Warner Books, 1996.

Kuhn, Thomas S. *The Structure of Scientific Revolutions*. Chicago: The University of Chicago Press, 1996.

MacKay, Charles. *Extraordinary Popular Delusions and the Madness of Crowds*. New York: Crown Publishers, 1980.

McCarthy, Jim. *Dynamics of Software Development*. Redmond, Washington: Microsoft Press, 1995.

Meyer, Marc H. and Alvin P. Lehnerd. *The Power of Product Platforms*. New York: Free Press, 1997.

Moore, Geoffrey A. *Inside the Tornado: Marketing Strategies from Silicon Valley's Cutting Edge*. New York: HarperCollins, 1995.

Nadler, David. *Champions of Change: How CEOs and Their Companies Are Mastering the Skills of Radical Change*. San Francisco: Jossey-Bass, 1998.

Nayak, P. Ranganath, and John M. Ketteringham. *Breakthroughs!* Amsterdam: Pfeiffer, 1994.

Norman, Donald A. *The Design of Everyday Things*. New York: Basic Books, 1988.

Ohmae, Kenichi. *The Borderless World: Power and Strategy in the Interlinked Economy*. New York: HarperCollins Publishers, 1990.

Panati, Charles. *Panati's Extraordinary Origins of Everyday Things*. New York: Harper & Row, 1989.

Peppers, Don, and Martha Rogers, Ph.D. *The One to One Future: Building Relationships One Customer at a Time*. New York: Doubleday, 1993.

Peters, Tom. *Circle of Innovation: You Can't Shrink Your Way to Greatness*. New York: Alfred A. Knopf, 1997.

Petroski, Henry. *The Evolution of Useful Things*. New York: Vintage Books, 1992.

Piattelli-Palmarini, Massimo. *Inevitable Illusions: How Mistakes of Reason Rule Our Minds*. New York: John Wiley & Sons, 1994.

Rapp, Stan and Thomas J. Collins. *Beyond Maximarketing: The New Power of Caring and Daring*. New York: McGraw-Hill, 1994.

Rapp, Stan, and Thomas J. Collins. *The New Maximarketing*. New York: McGraw-Hill, 1996.

Rich, Ben R., and Leo Janos. *Skunk Works*. Boston: Little, Brown, 1994.

RoAne, Susan. *The Secrets of Savvy Networking*. New York: Warner Books, 1993.

Robert, Michel. *Strategy Pure and Simple: How Winning CEOs Outthink Their Competition*. New York: McGraw-Hill, 1993.

Rogers, Alison. "Iacocca's Minivan." *Fortune*, 30 May 1994.

Russo, J. Edward. *Decision Traps: The Ten Barriers to Brilliant Decision-making and How to Overcome Them*. New York: Fireside, 1989.

Sapolsky, Robert. "On the Role of Upholstery in Cardiovascular Physiology." *Discover*, November 1997: 58–66.

Shapiro, Eileen C. *Fad Surfing in the Boardroom—Reclaiming the Courage to Manage in the Age of Instant Answers*. Reading, MA: Addison-Wesley Publishing Company, 1995.

Simon, Hermann. *Hidden Champions: Lessons from 500 of the World's Best Unknown Companies*. Boston: Harvard Business School Press, 1996.

Smith, Katherine Snow. "Organ breathes new life into Fletcher Music sales." *Tampa Bay Business Journal* 14, no. 23 (1994): 3.

Tedlow, Richard S. *New and Improved: The Story of Mass Marketing in America.* New York: Basic Books, 1990.

The Quotation Company. *The Manager's Book of Quotations.* New York: American Management Association, 1989.

Thomas, Bob. *Walt Disney: An American Original.* New York: Hyperion, 1994.

Trimble, Vance. *Overnight Success: Federal Express and Frederick Smith, Its Renegade Creator.* New York: Crown Publishers, Inc., 1993.

Tuchman, Barbara W. *The March of Folly: From Troy to Vietnam.* New York: Ballantine Books, 1984.

Utterback, James M. *Mastering the Dynamics of Innovation: How Companies Can Seize Opportunities in the Face of Technological Change.* Cambridge: Harvard Business School Press, 1994.

Whiteley Richard, and Diane Hessan. *Customer Centered Growth: Five Proven Strategies for Building Competitive Advantage.* Reading, Mass: Addison-Wesley, 1996.

Wujec, Tom. *Five Star Mind.* New York: Doubleday, 1995.

Yurko, Chris, "Wrecked Car? Call a Van." *Daily Hampshire Gazette,* 6 November 1996, 15.

Notes

And now let the weak say, "I am strong!"

Chapter 1: Cogita Differenter (Think Different)

1. My thanks to Holly Camerota for the Latin translation of "Think Different."

2. My thanks to Adam J. Bezark for this example.

3. Wroe Alderson, *Marketing Behavior and Executive Action* (Homewood, Ill.: Richard D. Irwin, 1957), 388–389.

4. Ronald Henkoff, "New Management Secrets from Japan—Really," *Fortune*, 27 November 1995, 135.

5. Massimo Piattelli-Palmarini, *Inevitable Illusions: How Mistakes of Reason Rule Our Minds* (New York: John Wiley & Sons, 1994), 57.

6. Alderson, *Marketing Behavior,* 390.

7. Gary Hamel, "Strategy as Revolution," *Harvard Business Review* 74, no. 4 (1996): 72.

8. René Descartes, *Discourse on Method, Optics, Geometry, and Meteorology* (Indianapolis: Bobbs-Merrill, 1965), quoted in *Marketing Behavior* by Wroe Alderson, 387.

9. Wilbur Wright, presentation to Western Society of Engineers, Dayton, Ohio, September 18, 1901.

10. My thanks to Dan Smith for this example.

11. David H. Freedman, "The Butterfly Solution," *Discover*, April 1997, 53.

12. My thanks to Tony Jacobs for this concept.

13. Tom Wujec, *Five Star Mind* (New York: Doubleday, 1995), 71.

14. Chris Yurko, "Wrecked Car? Call a Van," *Daily Hampshire Gazette*, 6 November 1996, 15.

15. My thanks to Ken Tidwell, Leon Mayeri, and Peter Jensen for each independently suggesting this example.

16. My thanks to Timothy Knox for this example.

17. My thanks to Rich Gay for this example.

18. W. Chan Kim and Renée Mauborgne, "Value Innovation: The Strategic Logic of High Growth," *Harvard Business Review* 75, no. 1 (1997): 107.

19. Stan Rapp and Thomas Collins, *Beyond Maximarketing*: *The New Power of Caring and Daring* (New York: McGraw-Hill, 1994), 38.

20. Joel Arthur Barker, *Future Edge Paradigms: The Business of Discovering the Future* (New York: HarperBusiness, 1993), 61.

21. My thanks to by Peter Meng for coming up with the term "entre-manure."

22. Robert Friedel, "The Accidental Inventor," *Discover*, October 1996.

23. Stephen Jay Gould, "Creating the Creators," *Discover*, October 1996, 44–45.

Chapter 2: Don't Worry, Be Crappy

1. My thanks to Bill Cawthon for this example.

2. My thanks to Ken Tidwell for this example.

3. Jim McCarthy, *Dynamics of Software Development* (Redmond, Wash.: Microsoft Press, 1995), 55.

4. As coined by Brad Hutchings.

5. Marc H. Meyer and Alvin P. Lehnerd, *The Power of Product Platforms—Building Value and Cost Leadership* (New York: Free Press, 1997), 130.

6. Barbara Martinez, "Inside Job," *Wall Street Journal*, 21 May 1998, R23.

7. Thomas J. Allen, *Managing the Flow of Technology* (Cambridge: MIT Press, 1993), 236–240.

8. Henry Petroski, *The Evolution of Useful Things* (New York: Vintage Books, 1992), 22.

9. John Huey, "Nothing Is Impossible," *Fortune*, 23 September 1991, 134.

10. Alison Rogers, "Iacocca's Minivan," *Fortune*, 30 May 1994, 56.

11. Ibid., 56.

12. Bob Thomas, *Walt Disney: An American Original* (New York: Hyperion, 1994), 11.

13. Charles Panati, *Panati's Extraordinary Origins of Everyday Things* (New York: Harper and Row, 1989), 103.

14. Paul C. Judge and Stephen Baker, "Were Jim Manzi's Big Ideas Too Big?" *BusinessWeek*, 26 May 1997.

15. Richard S. Tedlow, *New and Improved: The Story of Mass Marketing in America* (New York: Basic Books, 1990), 262–263.

16. Daniel A. Wren and Ronald G. Greenwood, *Management Innovators: The People and Ideas That Have Shaped Modern Business* (New York: Oxford University Press, 1998), 59.

17. Justin Martin, "Ignore Your Customer: At Least That's What Some Smart Companies Like . . . " *Fortune*, 1 May 1995, 121.

18. Eileen C. Shapiro, *Fad Surfing in the Boardroom* (Reading, Mass.: Addison-Wesley Publishing, 1996), 129.

19. Ibid., 129.

20. Oliver E. Allen, "Kettering," *Invention and Technology* 12 (Fall 1996), 55.

21. Robert J. Kriegel and David Brandt, *Sacred Cows Make the Best Burgers: Developing Change* (New York: Warner Books, 1996), 38.

22. Christopher Cerf and Victor Navasky, *The Experts Speak— The Definitive Compendium of Authoritative Misinformation* (New York: Pantheon Books, 1984), 171.

23. My thanks to Dr. Thomas McMinn for this example.

24. Mark C. Fishman et al., *Medicine*, 2nd ed. (Philadelphia: J. B. Lippincott, 1985), 9.

25. Kenichi Ohmae, *The Borderless World: Management Lessons in the New Logic of the Global Marketplace* (New York: Harper Perennial, 1991), 33.

26. My thanks to Glenn Grafton for this example.

27. Ira Magaziner and Mark Patinkin, from a reprint of *The Silent War: Inside the Global Business Battles Shaping America's Future* (New York: Random House, 1989) 23–24 of reprint.

28. My thanks to Charles Schrey for this example.

29. My thanks to Brad Hutchings for this example.

Chapter 3: Churn, Baby, Churn

1. My thanks to Gary W. Henning for this great quote.

2. My thanks to Holly Anderson Camerota for this great quote.

3. My thanks to Peter Jensen for this concept.

4. More thanks to Adam J. Bezark for this tidbit.

5. David J. Benjack and J. Michael MacKeen, "MTV Networks: MTV," in *New Product Success Stories: Lessons from Leading Innovators* (New York: Wiley, 1995), 288.

6. From the Porsche Web site at <http://www.porsche.com/Creating.html>.

7. Clarence L. Johnson, *Kelly: More Than My Share of It All* (Washington, D.C.: Smithsonian Institution Press, 1985), 28.

8. My thanks to Roger M. Poor for this example.

9. My thanks to Bret A. Fausett for this example.

10. Hermann Simon, *Hidden Champions: Lessons from 500 of the World's Best Unknown Companies* (Boston: Harvard Business School Press, 1996), 115.

11. My thanks to Patrick Berry for this example.

12. Gould, "Creating the Creators," 52.

13. My thanks to Fred Weber for this example.

14. Michael Gersham, *Getting It Right the Second Time: How American Ingenuity Transformed Forty-Nine Marketing Failures into Some of Our Most Successful Products* (Reading, Mass.: Addison-Wesley Publishing, 1990), 238.

15. Jagdish N. Sheth, *Winning Back Your Market: The Inside Stories of the Companies That Did It* (New York: John Wiley & Sons, 1985), 129.

16. Jack Canfield et al., *Chicken Soup for the Soul at Work: 101 Stories of Courage, Compassion, and Creativity in the Workplace* (Deerfield Beach, Fla.: Health Communications, 1996), 134.

Chapter 4: Break Down the Barriers

1. <http://www.chasmgroup.com:80/library.html>

2. William Tivenan, *Encyclopedia of Consumer Brands*: "WD-40," p. 574.

3. Richard Whiteley and Diane Hessan, *Customer Centered Growth: Five Proven Strategies for Building Competitive Advantage* (Reading, Mass.: Addison-Wesley Publishing, 1996), 19.

4. Katherine Snow Smith, "Organ Breathes New Life Into Fletcher Music Sales," *Tampa Bay Business Journal* 14, no. 23 (1994): 3.

5. CNET STAFF, "Gates: Why Is Windows So Cheap?" October 3, 1997, 6:55 P.M. PT.

6. James H. Gilmore and B. Joseph Pine II, "The Four Faces of Mass Customization," *Harvard Business Review* 75, no. 1 (1997), 92.

7. James M. Utterback, *Mastering the Dynamics of Innovation* (Boston: Harvard Business School Press, 1994), 61.

8. Ibid., 66.

9. My thanks to Dave Towle for this example.

10. Geoffrey Moore, presentation at *Managing Change* at the Wexner Center for the Arts, Ohio State University, November 1996.

Chapter 5: Make Evangelists, Not Sales

1. My thanks to Charles Schrey for this example.

2. My thanks to John Brown for this concept.

3. Panati, *Panati's*, 163–164.

4. Ibid., 102.

5. Ibid., 206–207.

6. Gersham, *Getting It Right*, 238.

7. John 20:29.

Chapter 6: Avoid Death Magnets

1. My thanks to Jim Jones for assistance with this section.

2. Andrew Goldsmith, "Here's an Idea That's Not Quite Ripe," *Fast Company*, October-November 1997, 50.

3. David A. Aaker, *Managing Brand Equity—Capitalizing on the Value of a Brand Name* (New York: Free Press, 1991), 225.

4. My thanks to Gary W. Henning for this example.

5. Robert B. Cialdini, *Influence: The Psychology of Persuasion* (New York: William Morrow, 1984), 60–61.

6. Ibid., 61–62.

7. The term "hunting license" was coined by Al Ries.

8. Aaker, *Managing Brand Equity*, 225.

9. Bill Adler Jr. and Julie Houghton, *America's Stupidest Business Decisions* (New York: William Morrow, 1997), 54–55.

10. Ibid., 61–62.

11. Donald W. Hendon, *Classic Failures in Product Marketing: Marketing Principles Violations and How to Avoid Them* (New York: Quorum Books, 1992), 111.

12. My thanks to Patrick M. Gerrity for this example.

13. Cathy Anterasian, John L. Graham, and R. Bruce Money, "Are U.S. Managers Superstitious About Market Share," *Sloan Management Review* (Summer 1996), 68.

14. James Alley, "The Theory That Made Microsoft," *Fortune*, April 29, 1996, 66.

15. Barbara W. Tuchman, *The March of Folly: From Troy to Vietnam* (New York: Ballantine Books, 1984), 5.

16. Ibid., 7.

Chapter 7: Eat Like a Bird, Poop Like an Elephant

1. Robert Sapolsky, "On the Role of Upholstery in Cardiovascular Physiology," *Discover*, November 1997, 58–59, 62, 66.

2. Johny K. Johansson and Ikujiro Nonaka, *Relentless: The Japanese Way of Marketing* (New York: HarperCollins, 1996), 5.

3. Ibid., 41.

4. Johnson, *More,* 107–108.

5. My thanks to Bill Meade for this example.

6. My thanks to Brad Hutchings for this example.

7. Deschamps and Nayak, "Product Juggernauts," 80.

8. Don Peppers and Martha Rogers, *The One to One Future: Building Relationships One Customer at a Time* (New York: Doubleday, 1993), 100.

9. Cerf and Navasky, *The Experts Speak*, 231.

10. My thanks to Dr. Dale S. Rogers for this example.

11. Ben R. Rich and Leo Janos, *Skunk Works—A Personal Memoir of My Years at Lockheed,* (Boston: Little, Brown, 1994), 138.

12. Inspired by George Friedman et al., *The Intelligence Edge: How to Profit in the Information Age* (New York: Crown Publishers, 1997), 148–149.

13. Allen, *Managing the Flow*, 43.

14. Ibid., 126–127.

15. Ibid., 145–148.

16. My thanks to Rob Bair for this example.

17. My thanks to Leon Langan for this example.

18. Larry Downes and Chunka Mui, *Unleashing the Killer App— Digital Strategies for Market Dominance* (Boston: Harvard Business School Press, 1998), 205.

Chapter 8: Think Digital, Act Analog

1. Alessandra Bianchi, "Hands On CEO's Notebook," *Inc.* March 1998, 98.

2. My thanks to Ross Lambert for telling me this story about his teaching experiences in Alaska.

3. Robert Hiebler, Thomas Kelly, and Charles Ketteman, *Best Practices: Building Your Business with Customer-Focused Solutions* (New York: Simon & Schuster, 1998), 72.

4. Ibid., 186.

5. Another great tidbit from Adam J. Bezark.

6. My thanks to Nicholas Bernstein for this great story.

7. An online interview with John Hagel III and Arthur G. Armstrong at
<http://www.hbsp.harvard.edu/frames/groups/press/index.html>

Chapter 9: Don't Ask People to Do Something That You Wouldn't

1. My thanks to Christine Tripunitara for telling me this frightening story.

2. Tom Peters, *Circle of Innovation: You Can't Shrink Your Way to Greatness* (New York: Alfred A. Knopf, 1997), 127.

3. My thanks to Dave Bosshard for this example.

4. My thanks to Sean O'Shaughnessey for this example.

5. Brandenburger and Nalebuff, *Co-opetition*, 61.

6. Lisa Gubernick, "Granny Care and Kiddie Care," *Forbes*, 30 December 1996, 74–75.
<http://www.forbes.com/forbes/123096/5815074a.htm>

7. Kathleen Donnelly, "Belly Down," *San Jose Mercury News*, 16 March 1997, West section, p. 7. My thanks to Larry Rosenstein for this example.

8. My thanks to Mike Doell for this example.

9. My thanks to Paul Willemse for this example.

10. Malcolm Jones Jr., "Air Conditioning," *Newsweek Extra*, Winter 1997–98, 42–43.

Chapter 10: Don't Let Bozosity Grind You Down (*Ne Te Terant Molarii*)

1. Vance Trimble, *Overnight Success: Federal Express and Frederick Smith, Its Renegade Creator* (New York: Crown Publishers, 1993), 80.

2. Cialdini, *Influence*, 222.

3. Ibid., 230–232.

Index

An indexer must make certain that every pertinent statement in the book has been recorded in the index in such a way that the reader will be able to find without difficulty the information sought.

The Chicago Manual of Style

About the Authors

GUY KAWASAKI is CEO of garage.com, a Silicon Valley-based firm that assists high-technology start-ups find seed capital. Prior to taking this position, Kawasaki was the chief evangelist of Apple Computer, Inc., and an Apple Fellow.

MICHELE MORENO was the coauthor of Guy Kawasaki's previous book, *How to Drive Your Competition Crazy*.